The **PATH** *Made* **CLEAR**

Discovering Your Life's Direction and Purpose

The PATH *Made* CLEAR

Discovering Your Life's Direction and Purpose

OPRAH WINFREY

PUBLISHED BY

FLATIRON
BOOKS
NEW YORK

AN
OPRAH
BOOK

PRODUCED BY

MELCHER
MEDIA

THE PATH MADE CLEAR. Copyright © 2019 Oprah Winfrey. All rights reserved. Printed in China.

FLATIRON
BOOKS
NEW YORK

For information, address Flatiron Books, 175 Fifth Avenue, New York, NY 10010. www.flatironbooks.com

Our books may be purchased in bulk for promotional, educational, or business use. Please contact your local bookseller or the Macmillan Corporate and Premium Sales Department at 1-800-221-7945, extension 5442, or by email at MacmillanSpecialMarkets@macmillan.com.

An extension of this copyright page appears on page 207.

The Library of Congress Cataloging-in-Publication Data is available upon request.

ISBN 978-1-250-30750-7 (paper over board)
ISBN 978-1-250-30751-4 (ebook)

MELCHER
MEDIA

Produced by Melcher Media
124 West 13th Street
New York, NY 10011
www.melcher.com

Contributing editorial: Jenna Kostelnik Utley
Interior design: Jordan Wannemacher

First Edition: March 2019

10 9 8 7 6 5 4 3 2 1

To the teachers who help us realize we can take on the world.

CONTENTS

*There is no greater
gift you can give or
receive than to honor
your calling. It's why
you were born. And
how you become
most truly alive.*

—Oprah

INTRODUCTION

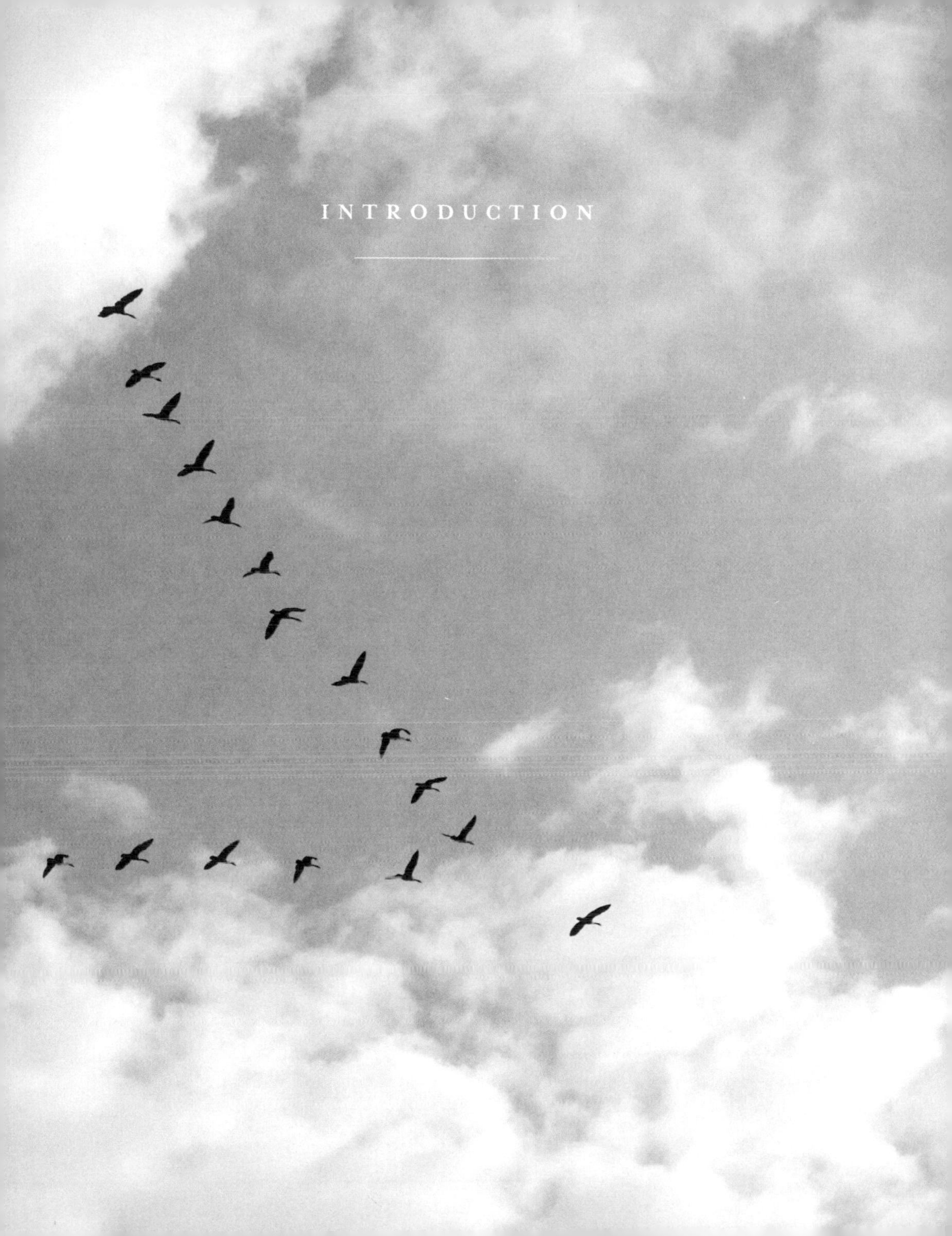

The simple act of asking "What is my purpose?" on the Internet has the power to elicit nearly one *billion* responses.

That's a staggering commentary on the way so many people feel about who they are and how much they long for an existence that matters.

On the surface, typing those four little words ... *what—is—my—purpose* ... and pressing Enter may seem trivial, but it's really a profound reflection of an intimate prayer rising from the deepest part of the heart. It's asking to be acknowledged. Initiating that search is a sign that the journey toward an elevated life filled with meaning and character is ready to begin.

And here is the *great* news. Beyond the labyrinth of digital links, there is really just one being who holds the keys to unlock the answers to all that you were meant to become. That miraculous soul has been speaking your entire life. Of course I'm talking about you!

I believe every one of us is born with a purpose. No matter who you are, what you do, or how far you think you have to go, you have been tapped by a force greater than yourself to step into your God-given calling. This goes far beyond what you do to earn your living. I'm talking about a supreme moment of destiny, the reason you are here on earth.

Each one of us has an essential role in the whole of humanity. All you have to do is follow your path to answer the call.

In the words of the Chinese philosopher Lao-tzu, *A journey of a thousand miles begins with a single step.*

My hope with *The Path Made Clear* is to offer the wisdom of experience from the visionaries, artists, teachers, and trailblazers who have walked this road before you, and who have shared their inspiration and lessons with me. The common thread among them: They have discovered that in this world, there is no real *doing* without first *being*.

Within these pages, you will find a guide to activating every layer of the miracle that makes you uniquely you—and applying it to the life you envision.

Committing to a life of purpose takes courage. There was a time in my own life when I felt torn between who the world was telling me I should be and what I felt to be the truth of myself. Today, I know for sure what I'm here to do. That's because I started listening to my instincts and paying attention to the decisions I made each and every day.

If you're at a crossroads in your career or relationship, if you're struggling with finances, with addiction, or to take control of your health, the journey to lasting change begins with defining what matters most to you. All of us have a limited number of years here on earth. What do you want to do with yours? How do you want to spend your precious, ever-unfolding future? There's no need to waste another day wondering if there's more to life. There is. And it's yours for the finding.

When you're ready.

Oprah

Your life isn't about a big break. It's about taking one significant life-transforming step at a time.

—Oprah

CHAPTER ONE

THE SEEDS

August 14, 1978.

It was a Monday, my first day working on a Baltimore talk show called *People Are Talking*. It was also the last day I had a job.

Up until then, I'd been a news anchor and reporter. I knew I was not my authentic self. And my bosses certainly made no secret of their feelings. They told me I was the wrong color, the wrong size, and that I showed too much emotion. I've always said that the best part about that experience was meeting my best friend, Gayle, who was a production assistant at the same station.

I could feel I was misplaced. Even though the six o'clock news was a time slot most young journalists covet, I was never fully comfortable in that seat. And, when I look back at the tapes, I can still hear the pretend anchor voice I used on air.

It wasn't until I was unceremoniously "demoted" to cohost of *People Are Talking* that I experienced the first spark of what it means to become fully alive.

During the show, I interviewed Tom Carvel, the Carvel ice-cream man, and the actor who played Benny on *All My Children*. Not exactly glamorous, but as we talked, I felt lit up from the inside, like I had come home to myself. When the hour ended, there was a sense of knowing resonating within my heart and radiating to the hairs on the back of my neck. My entire body told me this was what I was supposed to do. As a reporter, I'd been exhausted all the time. I really had to drag myself in to work. But after one day on this local talk show, I was energized in a way that fueled every cell of my being.

There was no doubt that the seeds of what was to give my life meaning and purpose had been planted. That day, my "job" ended and my calling began.

Years later, *The Oprah Winfrey Show* would achieve a level of success no one could have predicted. It was an exhilarating experience. And yet, another little kernel of knowing was revealing itself to me. Even at the show's peak, I had a deep awareness that a supreme moment of destiny still awaited me. That's why, after twenty-five years, I trusted my instinct when it told me, *This isn't it. There's something else.* The show was my home, the audience was one of the great loves of my life, but I couldn't ignore the flicker of certainty telling me it was time to move on.

The years following the end of the show brought many unexpected possibilities, and I had some daunting moments when creating a new cable network, OWN. Stopping to consider my own advice of turning challenges into opportunities is what allowed

me to move forward.

This is the lesson I hope you take away from this chapter: Your life is not static. Every decision, setback, or triumph is an opportunity to identify the seeds of truth that make you the wondrous human being that you are. I'm not talking just about what you do for a living. When you pay attention to what feeds your energy, you move in the direction of the life for which you were intended. Trust that the Universe has a bigger, wider, deeper dream for you than you could ever imagine for yourself.

Growing up in the church, one of my favorite Bible parables was about the mustard seed: If you have faith, even if it's as little as a mustard seed, you can move mountains. Anything is possible. As a child, listening from my seat in church, this brought me so much comfort— just as it did when I was struggling as a reporter in Baltimore and as it still does today. The mustard seed is such a tiny speck of a thing. I am emboldened by the belief that all I need is a mustard seed of faith and no matter what, I am going to be all right.

As you begin to identify the seeds of knowing along your own path, the first question to ask yourself is, *What do I believe?*

Do you believe that you are worthy of happiness, success, abundance, fulfillment, peace, joy, and love?

What I know for sure is you become what you believe.

—*Oprah*

SUE MONK KIDD

I think life is a process. You wake up. Then you wake up some more. One self dies. Another is born. It's an evolution of consciousness. If you look at the way God created the world, it's always about a seed and a sprout and a flower. And then it goes back to seed. It's always about process and unfolding. We're on a journey of greater and greater consciousness, becoming more compassionate, more loving, and that is a lifelong spiraling process.

TIM STOREY

You are a mighty person in the making. You are a miracle in motion. Motion is movement. We're not there yet. But we're in motion. At all times, we are all going through recovery and discovery. Some people stop their lives because they are in recovery. But you should be in recovery and discovery at the same time.

Dr. SHEFALI TSABARY

Whether we like to recognize it or not, even the most unconscious person, against their greatest will, is on a process to evolve. Life gives us opportunity after opportunity to ask, *Is this my truest self?* *Or am I living the inauthentic self?* Becoming conscious means to recognize when that moment arrives. And it's coming and it's coming and it's coming.

Pastor A. R. BERNARD

OPRAH: *Do you believe that everybody has a calling?*

PASTOR A. R. BERNARD: Absolutely.

OPRAH: *How do we open ourselves to that calling? How can we be more open to hear and more open to find the path that is our calling?*

PASTOR BERNARD: First we have to believe that we do have a purpose. Every individual has a purpose. And when we begin to think that way, we will appreciate the sacredness of life. And not be destructive to any aspect of it. We'll respect people better. Too often people think purpose is that one thing for which I was born. But what happens if you achieve that at age twenty-seven? You have no reason to live beyond that. Purpose is dynamic. Purpose continues to be applied throughout your life. Because your gifts, your talents, and your abilities that are given to you by God remain consistent throughout your life. But how you apply that changes as you live life from one level to another and you go through stages of life.

I have a number of different callings. And I think it's possible to be called away from things I have been called to in the past. There are goodbyes as well as hellos in our callings. Because a calling doesn't have to be for a lifetime.

—*Barbara Brown Taylor*

ELIZABETH GILBERT

There are still huge swaths of women who never got the memo that their lives belong to them.

There's this instinct that they need a permission slip from the principal's office for anything. You are allowed to ask yourself some really important questions about your life. You are allowed to take accountability and ownership for your own journey. You're allowed to ask what serves you. I know you've been trained up to serve everyone. But you're allowed to turn that on yourself and honor your own life that you were given.

Here's the question. *What have I come here to do with my life?* That's the question that begins every single quest. *What have I come here to do with my life?* There's no one who hasn't had that question come to them. That's the call. Now, you can choose to ignore that question or you can pursue it. And the pursuit is the beginning of the journey.

Bishop T. D. JAKES

If we can get the clutter out of our mind, if we can get the guilt out of our mind, if we can get the shame out of our mind, if we can get the worry out of our mind, if we can get the busyness out of our mind, then all of a sudden we're going to have ideas which are seeds. And the seed of an idea gets planted firmly in your mind when you believe in yourself and you believe in your potential.

The soul is the lure of our becoming.
We are coded in our cells. We are
coded in our hearts. We are coded
in our becoming. And we are God's
seeds, becoming God's selves.

—*Jean Houston*

CAROLINE MYSS

If you have life, you have purpose. If you have life, one drop of life. One. That is enough. One atom is as purposeful as our planet. What is in one is in the whole. It can't be otherwise. It cannot.

DEEPAK CHOPRA

If you're rested, if your mind is in peace, and if you're full of love and compassion, if you come from being and then feeling, and then self-reflection, then things will synchronistically fall into place. That's how nature functions. Like the seed. In every seed is the promise of thousands of forests. This is your karmic seed. *Harbam* means that you have unique gifts. Focus on the gifts. Don't focus on the weaknesses, because there are other people who will complement your weaknesses, and you will complement theirs. You recognize the gift when you're expressing yourself in that unique way, giving out your gifts, and you lose track of time.

I don't believe in coincidence. I know there is a divine order to the magnificent mystery of our lives.

Oprah

CHAPTER TWO

THE ROOTS

One of my greatest joys is watching someone experience an *aha* moment.

I delight in seeing that person's eyes light up with the spark of understanding. Especially when that recognition might change the trajectory of his or her life.

My hope at the start of every conversation is to expand hearts and to create an open space for learning. This is because I have always known that teaching is my true calling. It is the taproot from which all of my other skills and talents grow.

I felt this even when I was a little girl playing school in my grandmother's yard, trying to get my cousins Willie Mack and Lonnie to spell the Bible names Shadrach, Meshach, and Abednego correctly. Any chance I got to play teacher, I took.

Author James Hillman calls this the "oak within the acorn." We were created as individual acorns, in need of nourishment and proper conditions to help us grow into mighty oak trees.

I firmly believe it is no coincidence that I ended up sharing wisdom with millions in what became the world's largest classroom: *The Oprah Winfrey Show*. It wasn't kismet, serendipity, or even plain old luck. I don't believe in luck. For me, luck really means preparation meeting the moment of opportunity. I was born to teach. My only job was to listen, trust, and obey the call. The same is true for you.

In the following pages, you will read the stories of others who tapped into their unique essence, took a leap of faith, and now have a clear understanding of who they are and why they are here. Like me, they have come to know that there is no moving up and out in the world unless you are fully acquainted with the person you are meant to be.

What an unbelievable world we would live in if everyone were doing exactly what they were created to do.

A few years ago, I was talking about this very idea with Amy, my chief of staff. Amy's job is to keep all of the trains in my life on track, while at the same time juggling a wide assortment of daily curveballs thrown our way. It involves a whirlwind of multitasking. As Amy and I talked about recognizing one's early unique gifts, she had her own *aha*. She told me that when she was young, all she wanted for her eighth birthday was a filing cabinet. She just loved the idea of labeling the files and managing paperwork. She also had a calendar before there were events to write in it, and printed rainbow business cards so that people knew she could organize their lives. Now Amy's job is to organize me, and it makes me smile to see her delight when she's checking off a list. She followed her calling all the way to my office in Hollywood.

Of course, your purpose doesn't have to be tied to your career. I have many friends who told me they knew they were meant to have children before they even understood what it was to conceive. I've always believed that accepting the call to be a mother is the choice to become the ultimate spiritual teacher. Because mothers live in service and sacrifice to their children.

Whatever your calling, it's already rooted within you, and those roots can be trampled or tugged at but never removed. They grow stronger only when tended, nurtured—and, most important, shared with others.

My deepest desire is for people to get still enough to identify what makes them unique and connect to hope, possibility, and fulfillment in all areas of their life.

As author and spiritual trailblazer Gary Zukav so brilliantly taught me, when you align your personality with your purpose, no one can touch you.

—*Oprah*

NATE BERKUS

NATE BERKUS: I was the kid that cared so much about the things around me, cared so much about the way things looked, and more importantly the way things felt, that I was tortured by sharing a bedroom with my younger brother. For me it was my space, and my mother knew that. I don't think she knew that I would end up working in design. I don't think she knew that I would end up being on your show. I don't think that anyone predicts or dreams for that. But what she did know was that her son was the kind of person that had to control the way a space felt and the way a space looked. I would get great pleasure out of not just the privacy—that wasn't the point. It was the selection. It was the process. It was watching a space that was raw concrete walls in a basement be transformed into a space where I could live out my daily life.

OPRAH: *Because the space around you reflects your inner spiritual space.*

NATE: And I think it's universal. I think no matter who we are or what we have or we don't have, everybody wants to live better.

BRIAN GRAZER

OPRAH: *So, you weren't a great student.*

BRIAN GRAZER: No.

OPRAH: *And your mother was really upset with you because you were failing the third grade. Which is reason to be concerned.*

BRIAN: Yes. I was totally failing the third grade.

OPRAH: *But your grandmother wasn't worried.*

BRIAN: My grandmother wasn't worried. She liked all the questions I asked. And would always give me an answer. And she'd always say, "Brian, you're going to be special. You're going to use this curiosity. You're going to be a special kid."

And I was often looking at my report card while she's saying, "You're going to be special." My report card said all F's and D's. And I'm thinking, *What does she know? What's going on here? I'm getting all F's and she's telling me I'm going to be special.* But she just had this sustained belief in me and validated me for asking questions and for my curiosity.

I used this curiosity to meet new people in subjects that I would have never learned anything about. And by meeting these new people, it's given life to movies and television shows that I've done. It's helped me in my personal life with my children. It's been a powerful force in my life.

LIN-MANUEL MIRANDA

My parents both worked really hard. I have never known either of my parents to have just one job. They always had many jobs at once. And they worked so that my sister and I could have the things we wanted. I grew up aware of that. But I also grew up in a house where they were not around for the nine-to-five. We all ate dinner sort of at our own speed. I ate dinner when I got home. Sort of every person for himself.

They were there for the important stuff. They never missed a play. They were very present. But they weren't around. And so I had this enormously rich, imaginative life as my social media followers will see because there are hours of VHS videos and movies on there that I made growing up.

ELLEN DEGENERES

It was very clear to me that I saw things that other people didn't see. And I saw things that weren't valued, understood, or paid attention to. And that's why I became a comedian. Because I noticed the little spaces between the things that everybody else paid attention to. I paid attention to the stuff in between.

TRACY MORGAN

OPRAH: *When did you know that comedy was the way out for you?*

TRACY MORGAN: My dad was funny. He was Richard Pryor funny. He was so funny, I didn't really stay around my friends. I hung out with my dad and his friends. Because the conversations between his friends and him were more stimulating. I couldn't learn from my friends. They knew what I knew. But I could learn from my father and his friends. I remember when he came to the projects, everybody came out because Jimmy's here. And I remember him sitting me on his lap at four. He'd say to me, "Say, 'Your mother is …'" this and that. And I'd repeat back, "Your mother …" And everybody started laughing. And I liked that. And that's how far back it went. It was my dad.

Sister JOAN CHITTISTER

OPRAH: *I've never quite met anybody who knew at three years old, standing looking in a casket, that being a nun was their calling. Can you tell me how you knew that?*

SISTER JOAN CHITTISTER: My father had died. He was twenty-three. My mother was a twenty-one-year-old widow with this little baby. Two and a half or so. And she dressed me to take me to the funeral parlor. Her brothers and sisters said, "You cannot take that child to a funeral parlor." But my mother said, "Her father died. She has to grieve like we do. She's going."

So she's holding me in front of the casket. I've got my little hands around her head. I can feel the tears. Her face is wet. I know something terrible has happened, but more so, I'm looking over her

shoulder at the end of the casket. I say, "Mama, what are those two things? What are those things? There, at the end." And my mother hugs me a little and she says, "Honey, those are the sisters. They are special friends of Daddy's and special friends of God's. They taught your daddy in high school. And they're going to stay here tonight. And when God comes for Daddy's soul, they're going to say, 'This is Joan's daddy, and he's very good. Take him straight to God.'"

And I said to myself, *I want to be one of those.* I thought that was the best job in the world. You just sit around waiting and angels come. And I spent the rest of my life racing across streets to say hello to nuns. "Hi, Sister. Hi, Sister." I went to a Catholic school and I was not disappointed. Those sisters were loving. They were smart. They were competent. And they became a model of womanhood for me. A long time before there was any language for it.

Reverend ED BACON

When I was five I was playing alone in a pine grove in south Georgia. And all of a sudden, I felt enveloped by warmth and light. And I heard, inaudibly in the deepest part of myself, *You are the most beloved creature in all of creation.* At the same time I got that message, I also heard, *And every other person is the most beloved creature in all of creation.* It is that experience of unconditional love that has so overwhelmed me and made my life what it is today.

RUPAUL CHARLES

OPRAH: *I knew that you were my kind of human when I first heard you say that we're all born naked and the rest is just drag. I have a different way of saying that idea, but I mean the same thing. We're all in these body suits and come up with these definitions and ideas about who we are. My favorite quote is from Pierre Teilhard de Chardin, who says,* We are spiritual beings having a human experience.

RUPAUL CHARLES: That's exactly right. I got that as a young kid, and I thought, *Is everybody getting that this is all kind of an illusion?*

OPRAH: *Do you remember the first time you thought that?*

RUPAUL: I remember when my parents were in the living room going crazy, you know, beating each other, and I knew this couldn't be right. But when I was about eleven years old, I found my tribe in *Monty Python's Flying Circus.* I thought, *Okay, they get it. They're irreverent. They're not taking anything seriously, and they're having fun. That's what this is all about.* I got it very early. My sisters also. You know, we laugh. That was our sanctuary. It was a place where could find some peace. I like the lighter things in life. I tend to go toward the light.

GLENNON DOYLE

I knew I needed a place to tell the truth and I started feeling this invitation to start writing. It felt like an annoying tap from God, saying, *Get off the couch and start writing.* But I ignored it. So one day I was passing the computer and I saw this thing called "25 Things You Don't Know About Me."

My friends were making lists about themselves and I thought, *Awesome. I can make a list.* So I sat down at the computer and typed my list.

Then, I walked away, and two hours later I came back and my list had been shared all these times and I had twenty-seven new e-mails. I thought, *Oh, I really should have read someone else's list before I did mine.* For example, my number six was: *I'm a recovering food and alcohol addict but I still find myself missing booze in the same twisted way*

that we can miss people who repeatedly beat us and leave us for dead.

All of mine were like that. But my friend Sarah's number six was: *My favorite snack food is hummus.*

And I wanted to die. I just wanted to take it all back. But then later that night I started opening those e-mails, and they were from people whom I had known my whole life, but I had never really known. Because these emails said things like, *Oh, my gosh, Glennon, I just read your list and I've been bulimic for twelve years and I've never told anyone. Glennon, I just read your list. My husband and I are struggling. We don't know where to turn. Glennon, I just read your list. My dad's depressed.* And on and on. And I thought, *This is interesting.* This truth telling is something that can unlock people. I felt connected. Like the real me to the real other people.

Vice President JOE BIDEN

OPRAH: *I read that ever since you were a little boy, you had a picture in your head of the kind of man that you wanted to be. Did you live up to your own expectations? Did you fulfill the vision or exceed the vision?*

VICE PRESIDENT JOE BIDEN: By and large I believe that I have ended up being the man I wanted to be, but it wasn't in terms of accomplishment. Because people usually translate that into, *As a young guy, I knew I wanted to be senator. Or, I knew I wanted to be president.* But that wasn't true. What was true was I wanted to live up to my parents' expectations. And I wanted to be that person that met my mother's standards. Being defined by my courage. I wanted to be that person who, no matter what happened, just got back up and kept going. I wanted to be that person who was loyal to people who were loyal to him.

WINTLEY PHIPPS

When you watch the things you dreamed of as a kid come to reality, those are moments of destiny. But I've realized that moments of destiny are moments for which you were created, but they're not the reason you were created. The reason for which we were created is to grow every day to more resemble, reflect, and reveal the character of the one who created us. Let me tell you, God is the ultimate dreamer, and when He dreams, He also dreams about us. He dreams about you. He dreams about me. And the most amazing thing that can happen in the life of a human being is to catch a glimpse of what God's been dreaming for you.

Passion whispers to you through your feelings, beckoning you toward your highest good.

—Oprah

CHAPTER THREE

THE WHISPERS

For me, the early days of 2018 will forever be marked by the devastating mudslides that swept through my community of Montecito, California.

At least twenty-one people perished in the powerful avalanche of earth and debris that surged down the mountains in the aftermath of deadly wildfires and torrential rain. As I watched my neighbors gather to grieve, link arms, and ultimately endure, I was reminded of how, in a flash, your entire life can be changed forever. Natural disasters, illness, accidents, and unexplained events—there are gut-wrenching moments occurring every day that can blindside even the most aware and bring us to our knees.

This experience has heightened my understanding of what "circumstances beyond our control" really means. And it has made me more attuned to what we truly have the power to control.

The mudslides were a phenomenon. There was no way to prevent the catastrophic tragedy that literally came crashing through people's front doors. But that's not the case for most personal struggles. Situations like job loss, financial problems, a painful breakup, or a chasm between you and your child might feel like a shock, but they rarely arrive without whispers along the way.

Over the years, I have taken every opportunity I could to share one of my most cherished spiritual principles: Your life is always speaking to you. It speaks in whispers, guiding you to your next right step. And in many situations, the whisper is also the first warning. It's a quiet nudge from deep within saying, *Hmm, something feels off.* A small voice that tells you, *This is no longer your place of belonging.* It's the pit in your stomach, or the pause before you speak. It's the shiver, the goosebumps that raise the hairs on the back of your neck.

Whatever form the whisper takes, it's not a coincidence. Your life is trying to tell you something.

Heeding these signs can open the doors to your personal evolution, pushing you toward your life's purpose. Ignoring them—sleepwalking through your life—is an invitation to chaos.

The examples you'll read on the following pages help illustrate both the miraculous and disastrous outcomes that can occur depending on how you respond to life's whispers.

I'm particularly struck by the conversation I had with author, speaker, wife, and mother Shauna Niequist. Shauna was married, raising two sons, and traveling the country with a full-time job when she realized she could no longer ignore the ever-increasing warning bells that the life she wanted did not resemble the life she had.

As we talked, Shauna shared how, in her case, the signs were both physical and spiritual. And how, by finally taking the time to listen to the call and create the changes she most needed, she found peace.

Life is about growth and change, and when you are no longer doing either, you've received your first whisper.

Pay attention to what makes you feel energized, connected, and stimulated. Follow your intuition, do what you love, and you will do more than succeed.

You will soar.

—Oprah

Bishop T. D. JAKES

When you are not using your life, your time, your energy, for your highest and best use, and something in the back of the brain is going, *Ding, ding, ding, ding!*—you're missing it. You're missing your life, your purpose, your passion, your excitement, your enthusiasm. I want to shake you, and rattle you, and stir you up to understand that every moment is a gift. Every second is a gift. Every thought is a gift. Every idea is a gift. Every opportunity is a gift. Everybody you meet is a gift. You are gifted with opportunities to begin to maximize what you've got.

SHAUNA NIEQUIST

SHAUNA NIEQUIST: If we went out to dinner and talked about the things that mattered to us most, I would say family matters so much to me. My spiritual life matters to me. A deep sense of connection with the people that I love matters. Play and memory making and adventure, that's who I am. But if you looked at my day-to-day life, you would say, frankly, who you are is actually exhausted. Isolated. Anxious. Not sleeping well. Always hustling to leave something early to come late to the next thing. I was skimming in all of my most important relationships. Hoping that they'd still be there when I got back from this thing or that thing. I was forced to realize that the gulf between the two lives was growing at quite a rapid rate.

(continued on next page)

47

Any journey like this has a million different plot points. A lot of warnings that you don't take heed of and they get louder and louder and louder. But I was starting to realize that I was avoiding silence and stillness at all costs. Thinking maybe I wasn't just busy from a scheduling standpoint. Maybe I was hiding from something. But I hadn't quite articulated that yet.

That all crystallized when our family went on a trip and people recommended a beach that they said was the best snorkeling ever. So I went with my son. He was eight at the time. We're holding hands. I mean, it's one of those picture-perfect parenting moments. Where you say, *This is it. I'm going to hold this in my heart forever*. But it was like I had two halves of my brain and two halves of my heart. I had this deep—I think the best word I can think of is self-loathing.

This sense of *I hate myself. I hate being myself. I'm the problem. I'm the problem with everything. I'm ruining everything*. This set of voices that didn't seem to have any bearing. I couldn't figure out why they were coming out at this point except I realized it was the only time I had been silent in as long as I could remember. Complete, total silence. Not my kids. Not my husband. Not my to-do list running in my mind. Not me running from one thing to another. Not a television show. Not a song on the radio. Complete total silence that I did not choose. And it was in that silence that I realized there are a lot of things that I've been running from, that I've been hiding from, and I've been using busyness sort of as a defense, as a barrier against facing, *Where are these feelings coming from? What are they about? What will it look like to heal them and bring them out into the light?*

OPRAH: *You loved your life on the outside, but had become someone you didn't want to be around ...*

SHAUNA: Yes, I was exhausted. And for me, my exhausted self is my worst self. I'm short-tempered. I'm anxious. I get controlling about stupid things. Things need to happen my way when I'm really, really tired.

OPRAH: *Something you said struck me: that you were productive, but you knew you were not well.*

SHAUNA: When I look back, I had migraines. I had vertigo. I had what our family affectionately termed the stress barfs. Where I would just throw up several times a week when I got anxious about something.

OPRAH: *You weren't sleeping.*

SHAUNA: I would wake up every day at three a.m. These are warning signs. I wasn't listening to my body. I wasn't listening to my soul. I was just continuing to work.

OPRAH: *So even when your body is saying something's wrong, you weren't paying attention. Because waking up and barfing is your body saying,* Hey! *Your body is trying to speak to you. I always think that everything is speaking to you all the time. Your life is speaking to you all the time. But even then, you couldn't hear it or you called it something else.*

SHAUNA: I think I was so invested in the perception of being known as a highly competent, responsible person. And that was so important to me that I sacrificed my physical health and my emotional health.

DANI SHAPIRO

DANI SHAPIRO: I was waking up at three o'clock in the morning, every morning, in this state of existential panic. I didn't know what was wrong, but there was this feeling that I was falling and that there was just nothing to catch me. And I intuitively knew that it had to do with a spiritual crisis.

OPRAH: *What's interesting is, you were feeling this sense of angst, this sense of urgency flooding your body all of the time, but at least you were feeling it. I think so many people are so disconnected and numbed by the routine of life, they don't even have an opportunity to stop and know what they're feeling. And that's why sometimes it's three o'clock in the morning when it's waking you up.*

DANI: I would get my whole day done, and check everything off every list that I had to do, and drive everywhere that I had to drive, and get dinner on the table, and answer e-mails, and just do all of the things in that endless kind of list. Then my head hits the pillow. I fall asleep, and something in my being was forcing me awake because it was a thing that I hadn't dealt with.

OPRAH: *You're blessed to have that restlessness, really.*

DANI: Yes, it's a gift. It's a wake-up call.

CAROLINE MYSS

CAROLINE MYSS: We have an intuitive voice in us. We are born intuitive. We are so intuitive that for most people, it's the source of their greatest suffering. Because people hear when they've betrayed themselves. People are very much aware when they are not honest with themselves. It's that voice that says, *You shouldn't have said that.* Or, *You know that's not right.*

OPRAH: *Meaning things like,* You're still with this person, but you should have left twelve years ago.

CAROLINE: This is the voice of your conscience. It's the voice of your gut instinct. It's the voice you don't want to hear that never turns off. This is the part that says, *You should push.* And, *You should do this.* So it's the part that keeps us

moving and turning the wheel of our life. It's also the part that says, *This is it. You've done everything you can. That's as far as you can go.* It will guide you. It will say, *This is it.*

OPRAH: *So what you're saying is exactly what I've always believed and how I've operated. Once you accept when you have done everything that you can do, you surrender it. Let it go to the power and energy that's greater than yourself.*

CAROLINE: That's it. You got to give it your all. Give it your best.

OPRAH: *And then not be attached to the outcome.*

CAROLINE: Totally. You got it.

ADYASHANTI

We're always living a life where we're chasing a sense of self which feels, underneath it, inauthentic. And then life becomes a compensation for not knowing who we are. It is almost like a wound within us when we get disconnected from the truth of our being. We do feel that. And then we're trying to fill it with love or approval or success or the million ways that we seek fulfillment from outside of ourselves. But no matter how much fulfillment we get, there's that place inside that until we've realized the truth of our being, we will feel estranged from our own being. And from each other.

JON KABAT-ZINN

JON KABAT-ZINN: What mindfulness is saying to all of us is, *Find your own way*. Listen to your own heart. Listen to your own longing. Because what we're really trying to do is live our life as if it really matters.

OPRAH: *Because it does matter.*

JON: It does.

CHERYL STRAYED

I glanced over and I saw these books on the shelf. *The Pacific Crest Trail Volume 1: California* was one of the books. I had never heard of the trail before. I had never gone backpacking before. I had done a lot of hiking and grown up in the wilderness of northern Minnesota, but something about this book called to me. So I turned it over and read the back. And it told the story of this amazing national scenic trail that went from Mexico to Canada through California, Oregon, and Washington. And along the spine of the Sierra Nevada and the Cascade Range. And it just seemed like such an important thing. Such a grand thing, such a significant thing. And I was none of those things at that moment in my life. I just knew that I wanted to attach myself to it. The best way for me to describe it is that something bloomed in my chest. I felt some sense of opening or wonder. I knew instinctively that the wilderness was the place that I felt most gathered.

PEMA CHÖDRÖN

PEMA CHÖDRÖN: My whole life I've had that instinct of what's forward. I don't know if that makes any sense, but ...

OPRAH: *It makes all the sense to me. I think everybody has patterns. And it's your job to figure out what your pattern is. Mine is I've learned as much as I can learn doing this one thing. Now I need to move forward.*

And it happens when I've learned as much as I can learn at that thing. And then something else opens itself.

PEMA: Somehow there's always forward.

OPRAH: *As long as there is still breath there's forward.*

AMY PURDY

Instead of people looking at me, hearing my story and thinking, *Oh that's inspiring,* I want people to be "inspired" to take action themselves. I've had all these little whispers in my life guiding me; the whispers have quieted down over the years because I believe I am now where I am meant to be.

U.S. Representative

JOHN LEWIS

We were ordinary human beings, ordinary people touched by what I like to call the spirit of history. Some force just grabbed us. People had to do something, people had to say something. If not, I don't think history would have been kind to us.

WES MOORE

Oftentimes I would think, *Oh, well, I'm just waiting on God to tell me where He wants me to go.* Like, *God, tell me. Tell me what it is You want me to do.* And I've come to a very clear understanding now. It's not that God's not talking to me. It's that for so long, I just haven't been listening. I've been allowing so much of the noise to cloud this conversation I'm supposed to be having. I've been so distracted while He's been sending messages this whole time.

I really believe that if I want
something, God has three answers.
It's either Yes; Yes, but not right
now; or No, because I have
something better in store for you.

—*Kerry Washington*

THOMAS MOORE

The ultimate care of the soul is being identified with the life that wants to live through you. So at any point, your life may give a hint that you should be moving on—maybe to a different job or even a different marriage. And if you hold back on that and say, "No, that would disrupt me," you would be deciding to say no to life. I think that's where the soul gets wounded most. Your individuality comes from your soul. Not from your head. It comes from allowing life to live through you.

I have a lot of things
to prove to myself.
One is that I can live
my life fearlessly.

—*Oprah*

CHAPTER FOUR

THE CLOUDS

I have been speaking in front of people since I was three-and-a-half years old, reciting what we called "Easter pieces" for the church.

I still remember one of my first passages:

Jesus rose on Easter day
Hallelujah Hallelujah
All the Angels did proclaim

The ladies sitting in the front row would say to my grand-mother, "Hattie Mae, this girl sure is a talking child." Eventually, I was invited to speak all of James Weldon Johnson's poetry from his book *God's Trombones: Seven Negro Sermons in Verse* in congregations all over Nashville.

From then on, no matter the size of the stage or who was watching, I had no fear of public speaking. In fact, it was in many ways where I felt most myself—another instance of the oak within the acorn.

That is, until I got the call from Harvard.

By this time, I had been speaking for over thirty years, around the world, in stadiums filled with tens of thousands of people and during television events watched by millions. But being asked to give the commencement speech for this 382-year-old Ivy League insti-tution was a milestone. I mean, there aren't too many girls from rural Mississippi who can say they they got to go to Harvard to talk. What an honor!

And what pressure. I felt a *lot* of pressure: the kind of internal angst that makes you sit down at the computer to write, take one look at the empty screen, close the computer, and say, *I'll get to this in a little bit.* Then worry about it more, set a deadline to work on it again, and, when the alarm goes off, find an excuse not to do it. You know how that goes.

Usually in times of uncertainty, my mantra is, *When you don't know what to do, do nothing and the answer will come.* But I was not uncertain. Every part of me wanted to give this speech.

I have also followed the guiding principle *Doubt means don't,* but again, this wasn't doubt.

This was fear.

Fear that I had nothing revelatory to teach these brilliant Harvard minds. That I had nothing to tell them that they hadn't heard before. And this fear manifested as procrastination. Which resulted in guilt.

Months later, during a conversation with the author Steven Pressfield, I was finally able to make sense of those feelings. Steven said: "The more important an activity is to your soul's evolution, the more resistance you will feel to it."

He explained that no matter the dream, the shadow of resistance is inevitable. It's like the yin and yang—you can't have the dream without the shadow. So, the more importance I placed on the Harvard speech, the stronger the resistance.

This was a big *aha* for me.

And it was incredibly comforting. It meant that there was no point in blaming myself for my anxiety, because what I was experiencing was actually a spiritual law. The worries running around in my head were nothing more than the natural force of negativity at work, the shadow that lives in all of us trying to convince us of our unworthiness: *You're not good enough. What do you think you've got to say to the kids at Harvard?* Understanding this changed everything. It was as though a cloud had lifted!

Steven's theory was a totally new way of looking at fear. For every dream, there is automatically going to be resistance. But your sheer will and desire can be stronger than the shadow. You get to decide. You get to declare, *I want this,* and confront the fear head-on.

As you'll see in the upcoming quotes and conversations, doubt, fear, and worry stem not only from the voices inside you; resistance can also come from those who love you most. They might give you myriad reasons not to pursue your dream. But remember, although often well-intentioned, even your closest allies are usually operating with their own agenda, whether they're aware of it or not.

As for my speech, I found my groove after I realized that you don't need to have gone to Harvard to speak to Harvard graduates. I loved my time in Cambridge, and I'm proud that I faced down those shadow beliefs.

Fear is real. We have all experienced it. And it can be a powerful roadblock. The true meaning of courage is to be afraid—and then, with your knees knocking and your heart racing, take the leap anyway.

Ready. Set. Go.

—*Oprah*

Most of us have two lives. The life we live and the unlived life within us. Between the two stands resistance.

—*Steven Pressfield*

IYANLA VANZANT

IYANLA VANZANT: I'm not fighting the world. I'm fighting that part of me that says, *You can't do that. Don't do that.* And there's a part of me that says, *Come on, we're going to do this.* And then the other part says, *Don't you remember what happened last time? Oh, you're going to do that. You can't do that.* It's in me. That is where the real battle is. That is where the crux and the core of trust comes in. Those two parts of us. The part of us that would rather stay broke, miserable, and complaining, living in the mediocrity.

OPRAH: *And why? Because we're afraid?*

IYANLA: Because we get to control it. We say, *I know how to be broke and poor and struggle and suffer and be angry. I know how to do that.* But when it comes to being open and vulnerable—because the core ingredient of trust is vulnerability—that's unfamiliar.

OPRAH: *There isn't a person in the world at some point who didn't say, I* just find it difficult to trust people. *But you say that's not really the issue.*

IYANLA: No. The real issue is trusting yourself. Trusting yourself that you're going to make the right choices. Trusting yourself that you can hear that voice and follow it. Trusting yourself. When people betray you, abandon you, don't acknowledge you, whatever, you will be okay.

OPRAH: *I love when you say, "When you live in trust and faith,* truly live it; what everyone else says and does becomes irrelevant."

IYANLA: It really does. You don't even hear it. But then again, that means that you've got to be willing sometimes to stand alone. You've got to be willing to piss some people off. You've got to be willing to look different. Sound different. Be different. And those are risks that many of us are not willing to take. Because we don't understand God. You trust yourself by knowing who you are. You trust God by understanding God's nature.

JOEL OSTEEN

When my dad died, he'd pastored our church for forty years. I'd grown up there. And so all of a sudden, I'm the new pastor. I felt like I was supposed to do it. It's just that destiny on the inside. I didn't know I would be successful. But I knew I was supposed to do it. I believe those are our tests of our faith. I took that step of faith for the first time on a Monday. I told everyone I would do it. And that was the most miserable week of my life. I couldn't sleep. I was already against myself, thinking, *Joel, you haven't been to seminary. You're going to get up there and look like a fool. What makes you think you can pastor the church after you've been behind the scenes for seventeen years?*

I got up there and I had to hold onto the podium. I was so nervous and talked so fast. My first thought was, *Why is everybody staring at me?* I'd never seen it from that point of view. And, as I started to minister, I thought, *I've got to be like my dad.* I mean, all these six thousand people, they've come every week for years and years, and if I don't teach like my dad and preach like my dad, I just felt it's not going to be right.

The first few months, I felt pressured to be him. Not in a bad sense, because I love my dad. But I felt like I needed to because that's what everybody expected of me. And it was about that time, three, four, five months in, I read a scripture that said, "David fulfilled his purpose for his generation." I felt like I heard something there. I thought, *Joel, your dad fulfilled his purpose. Go be you.*

I think you can talk yourself into your dreams, or you can talk yourself out of your dreams. I think not running your own race is probably another one of the biggest things that keeps people from their destiny. Because you can't run somebody else's race.

MITCH ALBOM

MITCH ALBOM: *Tuesdays with Morrie* was not supposed to be some kind of big book. It was a tiny little book that got turned down by most publishers. So many people told me, "It's a bad idea, it's depressing, you can't write anything like that. You're a sportswriter." I had one publisher who, while I was in the middle of telling him what I thought was so significant about Morrie, said, "Let me stop you. We're not going to take this book. And honestly, I don't think you even know what a memoir is. Why don't you come back in twenty years, and maybe you'll be old enough to write a good memoir." I remember leaving there thinking, *Why can't they just say no? They don't have to knock it down.*

OPRAH: *Wow.*

MITCH: I actually heard from them later. They were interested in something else that I was doing after I had some more success.

OPRAH: *And were you kind enough not to remind them?*

MITCH: I did not remind them. I also didn't go with them.

TIM STOREY

We only have twenty-four hours in a day. So you have a choice to walk with wise people and stack up more wisdom. Or you can become a companion of fools and your life will unravel.

Dr. SHEFALI TSABARY

I have adults in therapy in their forties and fifties terrified when they're facing bankruptcy or a divorce or when life throws a curve at them. It is because they believe they will be nothing and they're so afraid to confront that emptiness. Little realizing that just beneath emptiness is the vast expanse of their spirit.

CAROLINE MYSS

CAROLINE MYSS: To the people who are in despair, I would say to them, I need you to be fully present and appreciate all that is in your life right now. I would tell them, you had your life focused on something that didn't belong to you, and a path that didn't belong to you. Yes, you did, or you wouldn't be here. You locked in on something that did not belong to you. Someone that didn't belong to you. You didn't let go of a yesterday that didn't belong to you. You hung onto a rage that didn't belong to you and you wouldn't let it go. You lost track of being here, or something happened to you, and you said, "It shouldn't have happened to me." And you never got over it. I promise you that happened. When you finally said, "It's not my life. I don't know how I lost my purpose." But no, you didn't—you did not lose your purpose. What you lost was the sense that you thought certain things shouldn't happen to you and they did. As if you were excluded from the ordinary everyday things of life and you can't get over it. The number of times someone will say to themselves, "I want to get out of this circumstance, but I'm too afraid to take care of myself, so I will lie about how happy I am in this marriage." Or, "I will put up a front." Or, "I will lie about this." But they're betraying everything that's in their heart. They're betraying everything. When they say to me, "Am I on the right path?" I tell them, "Here's what's true. You're on your right path, you're just not managing it that well right now."

OPRAH: *You're never on the wrong path.*

CAROLINE: You're never on the wrong path. You're just not managing it well. You're making choices that are harming you. And that's why it's hurting right now. You're making unwise choices. And your intuition is trying to tell you that.

OPRAH: *You're making unwise choices, including the path that you're on right now.*

CAROLINE: And the way you're managing the path you're on is harming you. And when your life path begins to harm you, then we have to sit back and say, "You've taken a detour."

OPRAH: *You know I just had an* aha *listening to you. I love it when that happens to me. And it's because of your use of the word* betrayal. *I've often thought, having had the experience of being betrayed by a close member of my family years ago, I thought that was the worst. I believed there's nothing worse than being betrayed. And just hearing you talk about it today, I think there's nothing worse than betraying yourself. That the worst, most ultimate betrayal is the betrayal to yourself.*

INDIA.ARIE

INDIA.ARIE: The first year I went to the Grammys, it was really out of the blue because I hadn't sold that many albums but I got nominated for seven Grammys. And then the show came and I lost all of them. And it was this big conversation, all over the radio for years, years. You know, "Why … ?" and "How could she … ?"

OPRAH: *How could you be nominated for seven Grammys and not win one?*

INDIA: Yes. It ended up being called a shutout. I've heard people refer to it as "the India.Arie" or "What if you get India.Arie'd at the Grammys?" Like it's this thing. But I realize two things about that now. One is that it really was God's way of giving me a breakthrough, because I was on everybody's lips all of a sudden because I lost. And those people had love for me and compassion for me. So then my album sales shot up. The second thing I realized is that

I was scared of failing and I was scared of succeeding. At the time, I felt, *Well, maybe I'm not meant to have all of that. And maybe I didn't deserve it.* All that self-talk. When I first got those Grammy nominations, I was having chest pains when I really should have been celebrating and enjoying.

I know this is going to sound simple, but I really feel this: Your self-worth is your job. It's your sacred space to cultivate. Because there's always going to be somebody who comes along and says, "You're not thin enough," or, "Your hair's not *that* enough," or, "Your voice is not high enough," or, "You're not going to make it in the music industry because you don't sound like all the other girls." But if you can, remind yourself that they're wrong because you know you're on your path. Sometimes I just ask myself, *What would I do if I knew I was 100 percent worthy of this? What would I do?* Just ask, *What if?*

MICHAEL BERNARD BECKWITH

There's a shift that takes place when you're talking about the possibilities more than you're talking about your issues. With your issues, your energy goes into the lower frequencies. Doubt. Worry. Fear. Now you're in that sediment. You're in that dynamic. But if you start talking about possibility, even if you don't know how to get there, then your energy starts to go up. Ask a *what if* question.

What if all my needs were met? What would I be doing in my life? What if everything is really working together for my good? What if all the bad things that have happened in my life are leading me to activating some great potential in my experience? What if God really is on my side? You ask a *what if* question and you start to notice little tiny miracles happening in your life.

DEBBIE FORD

DEBBIE FORD: The shadow belief is always fear based. It's when we say, *I don't want to be like that.* Or, *I'll never be like my mother.* It's also a fear-based judgment when somebody says something to us and it has this jarring effect and makes us angry. We know it's our shadow, because otherwise we wouldn't care.

OPRAH: *And the ultimate shadow belief is that I'm not good enough, right?*

DEBBIE: I think that there are a couple of core shadow beliefs. *I'm not good enough. I'm unlovable.*

Another form of *I'm not good enough* is *I'm unworthy.* And I think women more than anybody have that innately inside of them. So those are three very powerful shadow beliefs that birth all the other ones that come along. It's not about resisting these beliefs, it's about embracing. And asking how do we feel strong enough no matter who we are? We're born with gifts that have been so suppressed that we can't allow that real self to emerge. And if you can't allow the dark to exist, then you can't allow the light.

MICHAEL SINGER

OPRAH: *What are we supposed to do when problems show up?*

MICHAEL SINGER: The moment it starts with that chitter-chatter, my first reaction inside is to relax and lean away. I lean away from the noise the mind is making. Because you're going to do one of two things once it starts: You're either going to lean into it and get involved, and let it pull you in—

OPRAH: *Yes, which is what most of us do.*

MICHAEL: Right, or relax and lean away. And once you lean away and get some space, you will learn over time that that's the smartest thing you ever did. Why? Because you gave the noise room to pass through and it does. It passes right through.

OPRAH: *Why are we so afraid of change?*

MICHAEL: What happens is we've gone into the mind and said, *I'm not okay. How does everything need to be for me to be okay?* And then we devote ourselves to trying to create the situation that we think will make us be okay. And when things start changing and don't match that model, then we get scared, because it looks like it's not going to work. Fear is a thing. You can either push it away or you can let it go. You can either avoid it and be scared of it or you can let it pass right through. Fear comes up out of your heart, that's a very natural thing; it's human. You are watching, you see it, but you have the right to relax and let it pass right through you. If you don't do that, you're going to try to fix it. You're going to try to control situations so you don't ever feel the fear, and it all starts to bother you. Eventually you'll forget your whole purpose and you'll just be scared. You just get scared.

OPRAH: *The alternative is to decide not to fight with life, but for some people that can feel like just giving up.*

MICHAEL: But you don't do that in any way, shape, or form. Life is a natural unfolding of reality. You're supposed to harmonize and work with it. You don't give up and let it take over. Like if you get on a horse and you're scared, you're not going to be a very good rider, right? But that doesn't mean you let the horse go wherever it wants. You learn how to interface and interact with life in a wholesome, participatory way. Letting go of fear is not letting go of life.

ELIZABETH GILBERT

This was my victory and my battle. All my demons, all my monsters that I'd been carrying around forever, the light came through and I realized, Oh, they're not demons. They're not monsters. They're not dragons. I've been making them more grandiose than they are. They're just the orphaned parts of me. They're just the fearful-est, most terrified parts of me. They are scared to death. And they are throwing temper tantrums because of their fear. And now I have to tell them that it's going to be okay. And they will all go to sleep. I am the mother of all of these parts of me. At one point, I remember in my mind ascending above them all and saying, *I love you, fear, and now you go to sleep. I love you, anger, you're part of me. Go to sleep. It's fine. I'm in charge now. I love you, shame. Even you. Come into my heart. Go to sleep. You're safe. I love you. I'm not leaving you. You're part of me. You're part of the family. You're never going to be away from me. I love you, failure. Come into my heart. Rest. You're so tired. You're so scared. You're just children. You don't know how the world works. I love all of you. I have space for all of you. And together, we're just going to go forward now.*

All dreams start from the core.
Unless you are in total alignment
with whatever you envision,
the dream will get derailed.
Your intention has to be pure.

—Oprah

CHAPTER FIVE

THE MAP

How many times have you witnessed someone get close to achieving a goal, only to see it all suddenly fall apart?

Or, he or she does reach the top of the mountain but can't hold on. Maybe you too have struggled with near-misses and not-quite-realized dreams, yet are unable to pinpoint why. Self-sabotage can be a devastating cycle.

I believe deeply in what Paulo Coelho so famously wrote in his seminal book, *The Alchemist*: *When you want something, all the Universe conspires in helping you to achieve it.*

Time and again, I have seen how the Universe rises up to meet the vision that lives inside us. But just as often, I've seen dreams crushed.

The variable between winning the race and faltering at the finish line lies with one of the guiding forces in my life: intention.

Before you embark on any quest, you must first articulate your vision. Set your course. It doesn't have to be a public or formal declaration, but it does need to be clear. Particularly in today's climate, where there is a palpable craving for meaning and authenticity. People can feel what's real and what's not. So if you want support for your idea, stand in what you hold sacred. Those who sense your truth will rise up. And, most important, you must believe with your whole heart that you are capable of achieving your goal. If not, your path becomes murky and the goal stays out of reach.

For me, the journey to open The Oprah Winfrey Leadership Academy for Girls was one of the most challenging and ultimately rewarding I've ever experienced. This was something I felt I had been growing toward my entire life. I recognized myself in the face of each and every girl yearning to overcome the trauma of poverty and all that it encompassed. These strong, talented future leaders could see their way forward but needed an environment in which to thrive. That's why, despite confronting formidable obstacles along the way, breaking ground on the fifty-two-acre campus just outside Johannesburg, South Africa, was an important full circle for me. It's taken an enormous emotional and financial investment, but ever since the year 2002, when I shared with Nelson Mandela my hope of creating access to education for those who demonstrated promise and potential, my commitment to the school has never wavered.

So you can imagine my surprise when I was asked, during an interview, about critics who said the school would not last.

"They said that?" I asked the reporter.

"Yes, in the beginning," she replied.

My response to her was this: "People have no idea of my tenacity. Once I commit to something and I have a full-hearted desire to see it work, I can't imagine what it would take to make me quit."

I held a vision for what this school could be—a place to build leaders and inspire greatness. I handpicked every sock, every shoe, every door, every book—to honor the girls who would attend. The purity of that intention was aligned from my heart to my head. I had no ulterior motive. This was about bringing the power of choice to the first generation of apartheid-free women in South Africa.

That doesn't mean I didn't ask myself if it was worth it during some of the most difficult times. I certainly did wonder. But the answer that always came back was, *Yes, this is 1,000 percent worth it.*

I was convinced we could raise these girls to know for themselves what I've told them over and over again: *You are not your circumstances. You are your possibilities.*

In this chapter, it is my hope that you will gain a greater understanding of how discovering your purpose begins with committing to your course. Whether you want to fulfill a long-held dream, find greater success in the career you've chosen, give more of yourself to others, or repair a broken relationship, you must first ask yourself, *Why? What is the real intention?* And then ask, *How will I execute the action?*

The tenth anniversary of the Oprah Winfrey Leadership Academy for Girls was in 2017. To date, nearly four hundred graduates have gone on to attend universities around the world.

I set out to create a dream school where the brightest yet most vulnerable could find their voices and know for themselves that there is no bar. Their only limits are the ones *they* set. From day one I told them, "Don't just break the ceiling, reach for what's beyond."

As for the interview with the reporter who asked about naysayers? I went on to tell her, "Don't bet against me. You cannot defeat someone who knows who they truly are. I know who I am and why I am doing this, so I would not bet against me."

The moment you know with certainty that your intention is fully aligned with what you believe, all bets are off.

You've already won!

—Oprah

IYANLA VANZANT

If you don't have a vision, you're going to be stuck in what you know. And the only thing you know is what you've already seen. But a vision that grows inside of you, a vision that wakes with you, sleeps with you, moves with you, a vision that you can tap into on your worst days—that vision will pull you forward. Affirm your vision. Clarify your vision. Not only what you're doing, but also why you're doing it and how you're doing it day by day, moment by moment. And sometimes the how shows up only on a need-to-know basis. Sometimes you just have to walk blindly. But if you just do your vision every single day, putting one foot in front of the other, committed to your desires, being obedient, walking through your fears, the vision will unfold much grander than you could have ever even imagined or asked for.

Everyone is entitled to miracles.
And when they're not occurring,
something has gone wrong. We
have the capacity to lose the weight.
We have the capacity to earn
the money. We have the capacity
to live a far greater life than we
perceive we do. But we have to
make that decision. We have to
exercise that free will and make that
conscious choice to see differently.

—*Gabrielle Bernstein*

GARY ZUKAV

Your job and my job while here is to align our personalities with our souls. And we do that by becoming the personality that has the same intentions of the soul: harmony, cooperation, sharing, and reverence for life. Suppose, for example, you've got three children, and you're overwhelmed a lot. You can find yourself frustrated and/or exasperated by the child that's most demanding. You can find yourself angry at your spouse. What do you do? This is exactly the time to create authentic power, and here's how you do it. First, instead of acting on the impulse to tell the child, "Be quiet or you're going to go to your room for six months," or yelling at your spouse, instead go inside yourself. That's the first step. That is developing emotional awareness.

The second step: Once you can do this, you put yourself in a very powerful position. Because just by turning inward instead of acting in the moment, you have created a little gap between the impulse and the action. And into that space, you can inject consciousness. Into that space, you can do something you couldn't have done before. Choose consciously. You can decide, *I am going to say this to my spouse. He or she is insensitive and I'm sick and tired of it. But instead of reacting harshly, I'm going to act from the most loving part of my personality that I can reach for in that moment.* And it may be that the most loving part of your personality you can reach for is just not to say anything. But you have then changed your universe. It's your choice. And you make the choice every time you choose an intention. When you choose an intention of love instead of an intention of fear. That is the spiritual journey. That is the spiritual path.

BRENÉ BROWN

OPRAH: *You say that every home has to have its own manifesto. You wrote this one for your family?*

BRENÉ BROWN: Yes.

OPRAH: *I'd love to share this for people to incorporate as their own and adjust as they will. Will you read it?*

BRENÉ: Above all else, I want you to know that you are loved and lovable. You will learn this from my words and my actions; the lessons on love are in how I treat you and how I treat myself. I want you to engage with the world from a place of worthiness. You will learn that you are worthy of love, belonging, and joy every time you see me practice self-compassion and embrace my own imperfections. We will practice courage in our family by showing up, letting ourselves be seen, and honoring vulnerability. We'll share our stories of struggle and strength. There will always be room in our home for both. We will teach you compassion by practicing compassion with ourselves first, then with each other. I want you to know joy so together we'll practice gratitude. I want you to feel joy so together we'll learn how to be vulnerable. Together we'll cry and face fear and grief. I will want to take away your pain, but instead I will sit with you and teach you how to feel it. We will laugh and sing and dance and create. We will always have permission to be ourselves with each other, no matter what. You will always belong here. As you begin your wholehearted journey, the greatest gift that I can give to you is to live and love with my whole heart and to dare greatly. I will not teach or love or show you anything perfectly, but I will let you see me and I will always hold sacred the gift of seeing you, truly, deeply seeing you.

OPRAH: *I just wish everybody could live by those words.*

BRENÉ: Me too.

OPRAH: *That's how you change the world.*

BRENÉ: I believe it.

STEPHEN COLBERT

STEPHEN COLBERT: Spike Jonze, the director and a pretty good actor, too, came by and said, "Do you need any help starting your show?" And I'm, like, "Sure, let's talk." So he came by and interviewed me six months before my show went on the air about what I wanted the show to be. After we'd been on the air for a while, he sent those notes back to me and said, "I wanted to remind you what your intention was." And one of the things that he circled and pointed out in it was when I said, "I don't know how to do a nightly comedy show that's also about love. But I'd like it in some way to be about love."

OPRAH: *I think it's interesting that you set an intention for it. I live by that principle.*

STEPHEN: Yes. The hope is for love. And I think now we found that I love my country, I love science, I love facts, I love people regardless of their race or their gender identity. The challenge now is to love the people who don't seem to have that value in their heart.

DAVID BROOKS

In character building, there's a central piece of us that makes decisions. And every time you make a decision or have an experience, you turn that core piece of yourself into something slightly more elevated or something more degraded. If you make disciplined choices, you slowly engrave a certain set of habits and dispositions inside that core piece. If you make fragmented decisions, you make that core piece a little degraded. When I look at people with character, what they have is consistency over time.

Vice President JOE BIDEN

I think the reason people abuse power is that they are seduced by the notion that they are so self-important. That they really matter. When, in fact, it is not usually the case. The leaders I've observed who are the best are the ones who have courage to take a chance and be willing to lose on principle. And they are self-aware. They understand their strengths and they understand their weaknesses. They play to their strengths, and they try to shore up their weaknesses. The people who don't do that, who aren't self-aware—that abuse of power ends up in their downfall.

JEFF WEINER

Management is telling somebody what to do. Leadership is inspiring them to do it. And inspiration, for me, comes from three areas. It's the clarity of one's vision, the courage of one's conviction, and the ability to effectively communicate both of those things.

MARIANNE WILLIAMSON

I always talk about how, before you go into a meeting, just blast everybody with love. So, if you're going to an audition, if you're going into an interview for a job, blast them with love. Because if you have the thought, *Oh my God, I need this job, I really need it, and I hope they'll like me*, all of that actually limits your capacity to shine in the ways that might promote their wanting you to work for their company. So if you instead think, *The only thing going on here is I'm going to bless that person. And they're here to bless me. I don't know if I'm supposed to get that job. My only agenda is that God's will be done*, it will all unfold perfectly.

What are you here to do?
What are you uniquely good at?
Add to that the importance
of doing it persistently, being
dogged. There are massive
returns to doggedness.

—*Daniel Pink*

CAROLE BAYER SAGER

I've always believed in my heart that the best songs, the ones that resonate in my soul and therefore go out into the world and resonate in other people's, don't come from us. They come through us. And I always say a little prayer before I go into my music room. It's sort of a prayer of intention that says, *Please let me bring forth something that will help heal.*

CHERYL STRAYED

One of the most important lessons I learned through the success of *Wild* is that if you take that risk, if you take that chance, if you tell the truest, hardest, deepest story that you have within you, you're not going to step into the light and find that you're there alone. You're going to be surrounded by people who are there with you. Saying, *Me too*. When you take that risk, essentially you're risking vulnerability. You're risking showing your truest nature.

MICHAEL BERNARD BECKWITH

Potential is always bigger than the problem. Your potential is infinite and is always bigger than whatever problem you're going through. And your life begins to be okay when you wake up in the morning, and say, *I'm going to walk in the direction of my purpose. I'm going to walk in the direction of my vision.* You're being pulled more by joy. That doesn't mean you're not going to have challenges. We're not praying to have a challenge-free life. We're praying that the challenges that come will activate latent potential. You begin to see, visualize, the kind of life you want to live. Begin to write it down. Begin to dream about it. And then you talk about it. It doesn't mean you talk to every-body, because everyone is not trustworthy. You talk to selected friends. You actually talk to the vision. Talk to the possibility. Talk to love. You talk to peace. You talk to it. And then after a while, you're talking *from* it.

DEVON FRANKLIN *and* MEAGAN GOOD

MEAGAN GOOD: When DeVon and I reconnected on the movie *Jumping the Broom*, I remember thinking, *Wow, that's the kind of guy I wish I could marry. He's so amazing.* Damage I accumulated from childhood and past relationships had me thinking, *He's out of my league,* because of how amazing he was. At the same time, I felt God telling me, *It's time for you to focus on Me.* And so I did that. I started to focus on me and on God. And in that time, I prayed more and connected to God in a deeper way. I was praying for help. I was praying for growth. I was praying for healing. I was praying for maturity. So I spent the next nine months really finding myself, because even at that time, I was making mistakes in terms of putting myself in a bad position where I wasn't happy with the

results I was getting in my life. In both relationships and emotionally, which bled over into every other area of my life. It wasn't until a few months down the line that I got the revelation that DeVon was the man I was going to marry and, after focusing on myself and God, that I started telling friends and family that DeVon was my husband. Everyone was like, "You sound crazy."

DEVON FRANKLIN: Now, we had not started dating. I didn't know any of this at all.

OPRAH: *So you called this in.*

DEVON: She sure did.

MEAGAN: Yes. It felt like a confirmation.

JANET MOCK

JANET MOCK: When I was in second grade and we were asked, "What do you want to be when you grow up?" I said I wanted to be a secretary. Because to me, from what I learned in my culture, that's what women did. Women assisted men in their dreams. And then I went home with a note to my father from my teacher, and I thought he was going to praise me, but instead it was something like, "I think this is something you should be paying more attention to." And that just triggered my father on so many levels. His own insecurities about his son.

OPRAH: *It triggered your father because now your father recognizes,* Not only do I see the femininity in my son, but now his teacher is sending me a note home.

JANET: Yes. And so everyone basically gets on board that we need to fix this. How do we get this out of this child? And so my father started lecturing me. It was my first lecture from my father about the way that I should act in the world. The way that I should be. Boys are not secretaries. Boys are football players. That's what they do.

OPRAH: *So then did you try to conform for them?*

JANET: Yes, I started compromising.

OPRAH: *But this is what's amazing to me: At fifteen years old, you made a decision that you were going to go to school as a girl. You went in to school your freshman year as Charles, and by your sophomore year you were Janet.*

JANET: I came back after ninth grade and I was like, *I am not going to present in a way that makes anyone else comfortable. I'm going to present in a way that makes me comfortable.* And so I had just been elected class treasurer, and so I stood on that stage the first day of school, our sophomore class, and I said, "Hello, everyone. I'm Janet."

OPRAH: *And did everyone just accept it?*

JANET: I wouldn't say accepted it. I think a lot of people tolerated it.

OPRAH: *I think that's pretty amazing.*

JANET: I marvel at it now. At that time, it seemed like the only possibility, the only pathway.

MINDY KALING

MINDY KALING: My mother told me, "Before you can say 'I love you,' you need to be able to say 'I.'" Which has been something that I have seen in my romantic relationships, my platonic relationships, my professional relationships. And that means, before you can give yourself to someone else, you need to know what you stand for.

OPRAH: *Whoa.*

MINDY: And anytime I have been in an unsuccessful relationship in my past, I have noticed, *Oh, it's because one of us was not able to say "I."*

OPRAH: *Meaning, to stand in the "I."*

MINDY: Stand in the "I."

GOLDIE HAWN

At eleven years old I made a very definitive decision. And my decision was that I wanted to be happy. Above and beyond anything I ever did in my life, I wanted to be happy. But I remember these grown-ups coming to me and saying, "Do you want to be a movie star when you grow up? Do you want to be a dancer? Do you want to be a professional dancer when you grow up? What do you want to be?" And I would say, "Happy." And they would look at me really weird. "No. We said what do you want to be?" And I said, "I want to be happy." That's really all I wanted. Talk about an intention. That's a better intention than a white picket fence.

Find your lane. Make space for the flow to show itself. Follow the natural rhythm of your life, and you will discover a force far greater than your own.

—*Oprah*

CHAPTER SIX

THE ROAD

If there is anyone who has fearlessly lived the highest, truest expression of herself, it is the feminist icon Gloria Steinem.

Without the brazen conviction of Gloria and those who stood shoulder to shoulder with her in the fight for gender equality, I know the opportunities available to all of us women would not exist. Gloria is, without a doubt, a mighty force.

The last time the two of us spoke, she offered her sage perspective on how she has moved through life with such razor-sharp clarity. Gloria told me she lives in what she calls a constant "on the road" state of mind. This way of thinking, she says, reminds her to stay open to learning, because travel "brings people out of their heads and into their hearts" and offers the promise of expanding the truth. Spiritually, the "on the road" philosophy keeps Gloria in the moment, feeling "boundaryless, spontaneous, and at one with everything."

She compared her approach to a bird in flight, riding on a current, perpetually focused on forward motion, at all times checking the direction of the wind, yet open to all possibilities.

"Birds find their flow," she told me, "like surfers catch their wave."

Gloria changed the course of history by staying present and moving with the cadence of the moment.

For me, that "on the road" philosophy is the definition of the word *flow*. It means first identifying and then trusting your own current, one that is in complete alignment with your life.

You might have heard athletes, artists, or musicians describe flow as being in the zone. They use phrases such as tunnel vision, complete calm, or ultra-focus. Some liken it to a spiritual experience—a state of consciousness in which time feels like it has slowed down or completely fallen away.

Most of us have been in the zone at some point in our own lives. It's that exhilarating stretch where everything seems to fall into place. The road ahead is clear, open, and smooth.

So then, what causes us to get off track or feel like we're suddenly hitting every bump along the way?

Basketball legend LeBron James is considered one of the most intensely focused competitors ever to play the game. I once asked LeBron what could possibly cause an MVP like him to lose his rhythm on the court. His response: "I get off my game when I start playing for others rather than playing for myself."

Yes! This is a universal truth. We fall off course the minute our intention shifts from following our heart to responding to what we think others believe. All of a sudden, life feels complicated.

That's because you've altered your efforts in the hope of im-

pressing someone else. The goal is to get back to living for yourself, to get back to your flow. And that is not a selfish thing. It's an honorable thing.

Like Gloria Steinem, you too have the power to seek the highest, truest expression of yourself. The critical word is *true*. Not just speaking the truth. *Being* your truth. How can you embody the most authentic version of you?

The lessons in this chapter are geared toward how, after setting your course, you allow life to carry you. I have learned that creating your own purpose-filled momentum is possible only when you give yourself the space, moment to moment, to focus on the next right choice.

And despite the inevitable distractions, when you find that sweet spot, living your truth takes on a breathtaking level of intensity.

That is the brilliance of flow.

—Oprah

DEEPAK CHOPRA

Everybody's looking for the future. They're never in the present. So when they arrive at the future, it's not there for them because they're not present for it. If you get the idea that this is the moment that you have, it is the only moment that you have, then you live in the present, and you move with the flow, because this is the point of arrival. Right now.

———

BARBARA BROWN TAYLOR

I think we'd like life to be a train. You get on, pick your destination, and get off when you reach it. But life actually turns out to be a sailboat instead. Every day you have to see where the wind is and check the currents and see if there's anybody else on the boat with you who can help out. The weather changes. The currents change and so does the wind. It's not a train ride, in other words.

It's not all about the destination and focusing on not being there yet—though you will be one day, when the train finally pulls into the station.

I have no argument with greatness. But if arriving at my great destination becomes an excuse for dismissing my life now because I haven't found that great purpose yet, that's a waste of a day, if not a life.

A lot of times people think, *Someday my path will start.* But whatever is happening in this moment is the path. You're already on it.

—*Marianne Williamson*

Bishop T. D. JAKES

BISHOP T. D. JAKES: Have you ever seen so many tired people in all of your life? I mean, everybody's tired. Thirty years old and exhausted, twenty-five-year-olds who can't get out of bed in the morning. You know why we're tired? Because we're pretending. It takes so much work to pretend. When you can really be who you are and find out where you fit and function from a place of comfort, then you stop working. You stop wrestling.

OPRAH: *It's about finding your flow.*

BISHOP JAKES: Absolutely. And when you get in it, that's a life-changing experience. Surrounding yourself with people you want to be like takes you to the next level because they are modeling the lifestyle that you are stepping into, rather than emulating the lifestyle you are stepping away from. Putting yourself in environments with people who are positive or doing what you're doing, whether it's starting a business, owning a company, managing a division—you need to run with people who have your current and who are in your flow. Do you see that? Do you see that?

SHONDA RHIMES

OPRAH: *Writing is your truth, would you say?*

SHONDA RHIMES: Absolutely.

OPRAH: *Tell me what happens. We've all heard about athletes having a zone. Is it a zone for you, too?*

SHONDA: I call it the hum. I get this hum in my head where I feel like I could write forever. Like a frequency where you go from exertion to exaltation. There's just an endless joy for me. Where I feel like I could write for the rest of my life. And I lose time and my assistant has to come in and say, "It's been five hours." It's really lovely, a real, true happiness. It's very pure for me.

OPRAH: *It's a spiritual practice.*

SHONDA: Yes, it is.

JAY-Z

Flow is becoming one with the music. You find someplace inside the music that you tuck in. And you don't get in the way of the groove. You insert yourself in the song as an instrument. You're no different than the horn, or the snare, or the bass, or the high hat. It's just smooth and it just flows. I love having that experience.

JUSTIN TIMBERLAKE

Practice and keep working when no one's looking. Get comfortable in it. So that when you step on that stage, you're ready. Then you can literally forget all of it and just be in the moment. And then, do something different. Do something original. Do something different every time.

Remember: The most important thing is not what's happening out there. What is primary is your state of consciousness at this moment. That determines what form the future will take. So the important thing to realize is that what happens to you is much less important than how you respond to what happens. That determines the way forward in your life.

—*Eckhart Tolle*

JOEL OSTEEN

Be satisfied knowing this: If you're doing your best, if you're giving it your all, if you're pursuing your dreams, if you're growing, then you've got to believe your time is coming. And in the meantime, when we're content, we're honoring God. If you don't get happy where you are, you probably won't get to where you want to be. And so you've got to come back and say,

Okay, you know what? I'm not going on a big vacation yet, but I'm going to be faithful right where I am. I'm going to make good choices. I'm going to develop my gifts. And I believe God will open up some of those doors. You're saying, *Hey, you know what, God? I want to do something greater with my life. Or, I want to pay this house off. Or, I want to start this business. But right now, I'm not going to be discontent where I am.*

Brother DAVID STEINDL-RAST

OPRAH: *I think that what you just said is the key that unlocks the path to a successful life. And that is: Trust life.*

BROTHER DAVID STEINDL-RAST: That's the foundation of everything. *Even though I don't see it, I trust that life will give me good things.*

With trust, there is also hope. And "hope" is something very different from "our hopes." Because our hopes are always something that we can imagine. But hope in the spiritual sense is openness for surprise for that which you cannot imagine.

Funny thing about a mountain:
It always looks easier to climb
when you're at the foot of it.

—*Oprah*

CHAPTER SEVEN

THE CLIMB

In 2012, I had the honor of interviewing Valerie Simpson just after she'd lost her husband of thirty-eight years, Nick Ashford.

Better known as the legendary songwriting duo Ashford & Simpson, they had a four-decade musical partnership that produced some of the most memorable hits ever to come out of Motown. During our emotional conversation, Valerie shared the real story behind one of their greatest songs, "Ain't No Mountain High Enough." Sing along if you'd like ...

Ain't no mountain high enough
Ain't no valley low enough
Ain't no river wide enough
To keep me from getting to you babe

Most people think of these as enduring words of love, expressing the deepest form of devotion.

But as we talked, Valerie told me that when Nick originally wrote the lyrics, he was referring to his all-encompassing goal to one day write songs professionally. At the time, Nick was an unknown musician living in New York City, hoping to be discovered. While looking up at the skyscrapers towering above him, he came up with the phrase *ain't no mountain high enough* to convey just how determined he was that *nothing* was going to keep him from his dream:

No wind, no rain
Or winter's cold can stop me baby,
'Cause you are my goal.

And he was right. "Ain't No Mountain High Enough" now holds a place in the Grammy Hall of Fame.

I have always thought a mountain is a magnificent metaphor for life. From a distance, the ascent looks clear and smooth, but once you actually set out for the summit, you discover unexpected valleys and precarious ridges along the way. If your internal compass isn't set to keep climbing, every stumble will give you an excuse to turn back.

Over the years, there have absolutely been times when I've found myself climbing a steep, rocky road. Earlier, I shared the fears I struggled with when I was invited to give the commencement address at Harvard in 2013. I know my trepidation might seem surprising given the general perception of my career—after twenty-five years on a number one show, I had by most standards reached the summit. However, it just so happened that when Harvard's then president, Drew Faust, called with her once-in-a-lifetime offer, I was in the midst of one of the biggest climbs of my life. I'd even started calling this new endeavor "my Kilimanjaro." And in this particular instance, it seemed, the higher I hiked, the trickier the terrain.

At the time, I said I was "getting my butt kicked" in the news over the way OWN—the Oprah Winfrey Network—was "struggling," as they reported it. It felt like everywhere I looked, critics were taking me to task for OWN's performance. One of the toughest headlines announced, "Oprah Winfrey Isn't Quite Holding Her OWN." That one stung. I had enjoyed a long stretch at the top and was proud to be known as a powerful businesswoman. Now it felt like every decision I made ended up on the nightly news crawl. And so when Harvard reached out, all I could think was, *What can I teach about success when I've stopped succeeding?* It was a frustrating time. And to be frank, I was embarrassed.

At one point, I was deliberating what to do while in the shower. It's not a myth that some people make their best decisions in the shower—there really is something about the warm spray and lack of distraction that helps crystallize your thoughts. And indeed, as the water cascaded down and I thought about that mountain metaphor, I decided I would immediately stop calling the experience of building my own network anything but a privilege. *I mean, really,* I told myself, *who gets to do this? It is the honor of a lifetime.* If you think about it, people all over the world dream of climbing Kilimanjaro.

The words to an old hymn started playing in my head: *Trouble don't last always.* I got out of the shower and thought, *This too shall pass, and I will be the better for it.*

One of my favorite lessons from Joel Osteen is, "What follows 'I am' is what we're inviting into our life." Meaning when you use phrases like, "I am exhausted," or, "I am overwhelmed," you are inviting exactly that kind of energy into your life. The moment I shifted my perspective from *I am struggling* to *I am honored,* my climb was transformed from an arduous trek into a still challenging but now stimulating

adventure, and my entire outlook changed. Ever since that time, whenever I've encountered a disruption, rather than allowing it to rattle me, I ask myself one of the most meaningful and productive questions there is: *What is this here to teach me?*

Today, OWN continues to evolve. Every day brings a new teachable moment. And I look back on each step of the journey with gratitude.

The insights I hope you will embrace in this chapter reflect the knowledge I try to impart to my girls in South Africa as they consider any worthwhile pursuit: "There will always be setbacks. What you are experiencing is a detour. It's not the end of the road. You've got to be prepared to fail up."

Most important, I teach the girls that everything that is happening to them is a means to help them evolve into who they are meant to become. Nothing is ever out of order.

So when their will is being tested and all seems lost, I advise them to stop, get still, and listen. Their heart will tell them the next right step. And once they figure it out, it's time to look around and ask themselves, *Who is standing with me in the gap?* Because what I discovered long ago is that when life is treating you well and it seems you can't go wrong, there will always be people who want to ride with you in the limo. But what you really want are the people who will take the bus with you when the limo breaks down.

As you make your way up *your* mountains, no matter how steep the climb, remember the words of Nick Ashford:

If you need me call me no matter
where you are
No matter how far don't worry baby
Just call my name I'll be there in
a hurry
You don't have to worry
'Cause baby there ain't no mountain
high enough

Your Kilimanjaro awaits.

—*Oprah*

ECKHART TOLLE

ECKHART TOLLE: Being challenged is a good thing. Let's look at
the nature of challenges. First of
all, if you look at your own life, you
may find that what look like obstacles to where you want to go, where
you want to be, what you want to
achieve, seem to arise almost con-
tinuously in the form of difficult
people or difficult situations. Some
people resent being challenged by
life. They think challenges should
not exist. But if you have lived for
long enough, at some point you
realize that the world isn't here to
make you happy. It can't do that.

OPRAH: *It's like what you say about
human evolution: It's not linear. Rather,
it's take two steps forward in your life
and one step back. And the farther back
you go, the more of a bounce you have to
move forward. Right?*

ECKHART: Yes. We definitely have
evolved in consciousness. But
it does not go in a straight line
upward. You regress, and then
you go forward. You regress, and
then you go forward a bit more. It
goes in cycles. We need the crisis.
There are two levels of truth. One
is to see the craziness of what's
happening now. And another is to
see, from a higher perspective, that
what's happening now is part of
our evolution.

OPRAH: *It needs to break down so that
something else can break through.*

ECKHART: Yes. That's right.

My mother used to say that during hardships in your life, try to look at this moment in the light of eternity. Try to see this how God might see it. Which is what we see right now, as opposed to the past or the future, which we can't affect in any way. You can try to see this present moment—whether it's good or bad, a hardship or a victory— with humility, with acceptance, and with love. You can't love something until you can accept it.

—*Stephen Colbert*

Vice President JOE BIDEN

A tractor trailer broadsided and killed my wife and daughter, and my two sons were badly injured. As we walked out of the hospital, my mother grabbed my hand and said, "Joey, out of everything horrible, something good will come if you look hard enough for it." I thought it was cruel at one point, but that was my mother's notion. We were taught just to get up. When you get knocked down, just get up. And move forward. When you think about it, so many people, without the kind of help that I had, do it every day. Right now, somebody's gone through something significantly worse than me, and they have nobody behind them, and they're getting up and they're moving. It gives me such overwhelming confidence in people. The ability to absorb pain and the spiritual reassurance that comes from knowing those we lost are still a part of us.

Father RICHARD ROHR

FATHER RICHARD ROHR: For a marriage to be successful, you've got to have someone who wants you to grow into who you really are. And if you don't have that, I have seen people become smaller after marriage. But love has to expand. It always has to expand. I believe we each create our private salvation project—what will make me wonderful, what will make me look beautiful and be admired? And every time people have to let go of that in its present form and reshape it, they say, "Darn, I based my life on that salvation project and now it's gone." You know? "I based my life on looking good or being a priest or being married. And now that's falling apart. That's dying." And you never go there voluntarily. You fall.

OPRAH: *Yes. So this happens when you go through a divorce. At first you fight it, and you think it's the worst thing that could ever happen to you. And then you come out the other side and you feel a greater sense of freedom and closer to your true self.*

FATHER ROHR: Yes, it might take you five years to get there. But you wake up one day and say, *My God, this is much better.*

OPRAH: *Or you lose your job.*

FATHER ROHR: Yes, or your reputation or your money. You know, all of those tragedies. That's the way the self expands. I'm sorry to say it's true, but it's true. It's all what you do with suffering. If you don't transform your suffering, Oprah, I always say, with 100 percent certitude, you will transmit your suffering to your family, your neighbors, even to your country.

ROB BELL

We always talk about marriage as a creative act. You're creating something new in the world. For many people, that becomes heavy. It becomes, *Well, let's just try to stay together*.

Duty. Obligation. As opposed to, *We get to make something with this life*. My wife, Kristen, and I now see that we get to go on an adventure and create something new. So every problem becomes not, *Oh my word. Are we going to make it?* But, *Well, look what came down the road today. I wonder what this will produce. I wonder what we'll learn through this*. It's just a shift in how you view life and life together. It's an adventure in which you actually get to create and cocreate a life.

ALANIS MORISSETTE

ALANIS MORISSETTE: I thought that all would be helped and healed and soothed by fame.

OPRAH: *Because you believed, When I get famous …*

ALANIS: I will be less lonely. And I will be understood and I will be loved and that love will go in and heal any of the broken parts.

OPRAH: *And the truth is, there's no difference between fame or, thoughts like, When I get thin, or, When I get rich, or, When I meet the right guy.*

ALANIS: When I get that job. Yes. When I have babies. When I retire.

OPRAH: *Then I will be happy. I will be healed. It's all the same thing.*

ALANIS: And everything will be okay. Yes. As though somehow we as humans could be exempt from pain. You know, one of the big lessons I've learned has been that if I can be comfortable with pain, which is different from suffering, but comfortable with pain as just an indication. And, it's potentially a daily thing, in my case, then there won't be my living in the future all the time. That one day if and when I'll be happy and that on the other side there is this great sense of peace.

CHERYL STRAYED

How long do we hold on to this old idea? I was going to do this job or I was going to go to this school or I was going to be married to this person. And it doesn't serve us anymore.

I once wrote a letter to my younger self and told the younger me, *It's okay to rewrite my story from time to time.* And not only okay, but necessary. Sometimes you have to see things through, even though they don't cause you joy. But sometimes you need to say, *You know what? I'm not going to surrender my joy. I'm not going to be this thing anymore. That story is no longer true. I'm going to be this other thing. This other way.*

TRACEY JACKSON

OPRAH: *Many times when you try to change, there's a whole circle of people who actually liked you better the old way. And a lot of people are torn between that life and the life that's calling for them.*

TRACEY JACKSON: You develop languages with people and you develop patterns of behavior. For instance: *I'm the dysfunctional one; you're the functional one. I'm the one in control. You're the one who's a little bit crazy. I'm always depressed.* Whatever it may be. But when you change that, all of a sudden their role in your life is put into question. And they start having to question their own behavior.

You don't have to do the shiny perfect thing. You can get through life by showing up and saying, *Okay, this is hard and I need help. I need a higher power. And I need you.*

—*Glennon Doyle*

TRACY MCMILLAN

The lesson that took me the longest to learn is that I have to practice hard-core compassion for myself. Because I used to be very hard on myself. I thought I was supposed to know things before it was possible to know them. And the truth is that every-thing we're doing, that's our life's work. My life's work is to learn how to love better. My life's work is to learn how to put light in places where it's dark.

CINDY CRAWFORD

The idea of getting older is daunting and intimidating and not that fun, really. But recently I shifted to *I have the privilege of getting older*, and I really like that because it's easy to spin off into the negative, as opposed to *Aren't we lucky?* That we're here, that we get to get older. I think it's a lot easier to see yourself getting older if you're happy in your life or if you're doing meaningful work, and you are contributing to life in a way that makes you feel good about yourself.

———

JON BON JOVI

Anytime you think you've hit the top of the mountain, the truth is, you've just reached another mountain, and it's there to climb over again. Each step along the way is just a life lesson in humility. And it gives you the ammunition to go on and be excited about the next day.

JOEL OSTEEN

What follows "I am" is what we're inviting into our life. You say "I am tired." "I am frustrated." "I am lonely." Well, now you've invited more of that in. So the principle is to turn it around and invite what you want into your life. There's a balance to it. I don't think you're denying the facts. You're just not magnifying the negative. Rather, start saying, "I am a masterpiece. I am fearfully and wonderfully made. I am strong. I am talented." I think that is speaking to the core of what God's put in each one of us. He has equipped us. He's empowered us. We have what we need to fulfill our destiny. But we have to bring it out. And you can't bring it out being against yourself.

My life's goal is to be of service to a greater good. Wherever that true calling takes me, I've always been willing to go.

—Oprah

CHAPTER EIGHT

THE GIVE

My spiritual queen mother, the great Maya Angelou, was for me the ultimate teacher.

Only Maya had the ability to reduce me to my seven-year-old self simply by the way she greeted me.

"Hello, you darling girl," she would say at the start of every conversation. Her e-mails always set a loving tone, opening with, *Oh Dearie O.*

I'll never forget the first time she shared with me what would later become a much beloved refrain: *People may not remember what you did or what you said, but they always remember how you made them feel.*

What her words so brilliantly remind us is that every single moment is an opportunity to be of service to another human being. That is what I hope will be your takeaway from this chapter. I'm not referring just to volunteering or contributing to a cause, though those are wonderful, worthwhile activities that strengthen us. What I am talking about is committing, decision by decision, to a sustained, heartfelt, compassionate approach to life.

We are more alike than we are different, Maya used to say.

Imagine what would happen if two people with opposing views came together to inform each other from a position of wanting to be of service. If you're caught in the deluge of negativity and vitriol we're bombarded with on a daily basis, this would seem a nearly impossible idea. But I believe we're closer to reconnecting than we realize.

When I accepted the Cecil B. DeMille Award at the 2018 Golden Globes, my speech caused a bit of a stir. It was not my intention to spark talk of a presidential campaign, but I can tell you why I believe that speech resonated with so many people. In my conversations with men and women from many walks of life, I have felt a growing shift, a mutual yearning on all sides for a different way of envisioning the world. There is an eagerness rising within all of us to bridge our divides, to bring an end to vicious attacks on those whose viewpoints differ from ours, and to focus on elevating humanity. What I was trying to express in my speech was that all humans have value and a voice. And I consider it my purpose here on earth to celebrate and validate both.

The sheer volume of reaction to what I said at the Golden Globes is a direct testament to the fact that millions of us are ready to seek out and stand up for what's good, right, and just in our world.

Maya once told me that my legacy will be every person whose life was touched by my being here. I believe the same is true for all of us. When it comes down to it, life can be measured in exchanges of energy. Positive or negative: What is the energy you choose to bring to the world? Positive exchanges multiply and grow. That's why giving on any level feels so great. You are creating an actual force for good.

Most people wait to assess their legacy until their second or third act of life, when there is time to sit back and reflect. But what if, right now, you began to structure your decisions based on how you want to be remembered, rather than on what you believe you still need to accomplish? What I'm suggesting is that you don't wait until you're sitting on your porch in your rocking chair to evaluate the character of your actions. Ask yourself today, in the middle of your complicated, demanding, chaotic life: *What do I want my legacy to be?* And then start living from that intention.

As Maya always said: *When you know, teach. When you get, give.*

—*Oprah*

I want my legacy to be that what matters most in this life moves through me the way air moves through a window to refresh another.

—*Mark Nepo*

BRYAN STEVENSON

Often we measure how we're doing in life by how much money we make or how many people know our name, and all these other kinds of metrics. I think there's another way of measuring how you're doing: by how many stones you catch. By how often you actually position yourself to help those who need help. There's something redemptive, powerful, and transformative about catching the stones that people throw at each other unfairly. We run from problems, most of us. But sometimes we have to run *to* the problem.

GLORIA STEINEM

If you are in a place where you're more powerful than the people around you, listen as much as you talk. And if you're less powerful, talk as much as you listen.

THICH NHAT HANH

Deep listening is the kind of listening that can help relieve the suffering of the other person. You can call it compassionate listening. You listen with only one purpose: Help him or her to empty their heart. Remember that you are helping him or her to suffer less, and even if they say things full of wrong perceptions, full of bitterness, you are still capable of continuing to listen with compassion. If you want to help them correct their perception, you wait for another time; at this time, you just listen with compassion and help him or her to suffer less. One hour like that can bring transformation and healing.

U.S. Representative
JOHN LEWIS

During the Freedom Rides, or during the sit-ins, during my civil-rights efforts in Mississippi, or working in Selma, I never ever thought about giving up and saying, *This is too much*. I never thought about dropping out. You come to that point where you're saying, *I've got to go on and see what the end's going to be*. You have to. You have to get out there and push and pull to try to make things better for a generation yet unborn. Each one of us has the ability to resist, not to be quiet. We have to be brave. We have to be bold. And sometimes you have to fight some of the old battles over and over again for the next generation. You too can make a contribution, and you must.

MARIANNE WILLIAMSON

OPRAH: *I think what's really important is to understand that in the making of history it's not the majority of people. Everybody's waiting on the majority to all agree that we need to move in a certain direction. But you say that is not the case.*

MARIANNE WILLIAMSON: The majority of people didn't wake up one day and go, "Let's free the slaves." The majority of people didn't wake up one day and say, "Let's give women the right to vote." It's because a small group of people usually considered outrageous radicals by the status quo of their day had a better idea. That's how evolution works.

DEEPAK CHOPRA

There's a body, there's a mind, and there's also a soul consciousness. When you get in touch with the soul consciousness, you become aware that other people also have a soul, and you communicate with that. Then you realize that you're both part of a more divine realm, and that's called "divine consciousness." You can go even deeper into what is then called "unity consciousness," where you realize that we are all inseparably one. All the separation is totally artificial.

CHARLES EISENSTEIN

CHARLES EISENSTEIN: We live in communities that aren't really communities because we don't know the people around us. We're surrounded by strangers. So we feel lonely. Our sense of being in the world depends on our relationships. I'm talking about really being known. When we don't know our neighbors and we're not participating in the natural world in an intimate way, then we feel alone. We don't even know who we are.

There's a deficit of identity when we're shrunk down into these little separate selves.

OPRAH: *Another word for suffering you use is separation, this feeling that you're disconnected, even though you are in a room, or in a world where you are engaging with people all the time, but there's this low-level sense of disconnection from community. That's what you're talking about. You say, "On some level, we all*

know better. This knowledge seldom finds clear articulation. So instead, we express it indirectly through covert and overt rebellion." I found that so interesting. "Addiction. Self-sabotage. Procrastination. Laziness. Rage. Chronic fatigue. And depression. All are ways that we withhold our full participation in the program of life that we are offered." Well said, sir.

CHARLES: You are the mirror of all things. You are the totality of your relationships. So that means that anything that happens to anything, to any being, is happening to you on some level. It means that any difficult relationship you have is mirroring something in yourself. It means that everything you do to the world will somehow come back to you. It means the world outside of ourselves is not just a bunch of stuff. But it's a mirror itself. It's happening to you. Everything that's happening to the world is happening to us. And whether or not we believe it, we can still feel it. That's why it hurts so much. And we don't even know why.

LYNNE TWIST

LYNNE TWIST: When you let go of trying to get more of what you don't really need, it frees up oceans of energy that was caught up in that chase to now turn and pay attention to what you already have. When you actually pay attention to, nourish, love, and share what you already have, it expands. It's the opposite of what we think. And when people know that, it frees them from this chase of more, more, more, more, more. A shorter way to say all that is, What you appreciate, appreciates.

OPRAH: *That is such a fantastic tweetable lesson. It's universal law, actually. What you focus on expands. What you appreciate, appreciates.*

LYNNE: Exactly. And the way we have that kind of experience is by sharing. By contributing. By serving. By nourishing other people. That's where real prosperity lives.

President JIMMY CARTER

Rosalynn and I spend a full week every year in some remote place building Habitat for Humanity houses. And one of the things I've learned is that when we work side by side with a family that's never had a decent home in their lives, we begin to comprehend quite clearly and vividly that their moral values are just as good as mine. And their ambitions are just as great as mine. We realize that just because somebody's poverty-stricken and deprived of what we look upon as successes in life—they're not inferior. That's a major lesson I've learned in my adult life, and particularly since I left the White House: that people are not inferior.

MINDY KALING

As a woman who's an employee, often you are the only woman. And you think, *There's not enough space for me*, or, *There's only going to be one Indian woman, there's only going to be one minority. I hope I'm it. I can't help anybody else.* Those are the terrible habits you learn when you're younger. But as an employer, you're like, *If I can stop that anxiety for young women, and tell them there isn't going to be only one Indian woman, one African American woman, one woman* period *in here, there's going to be space for lots, so you don't have to have that anxiety anymore.* That's one way I try to help.

Give to the world what you want
to receive from the world, because
that is what you will receive.

— *Gary Zukav*

The poet Daniel Ladinsky wrote, *Even after all this time, the sun never says to the earth, "You owe me." Look what happens with a love like that. It lights the whole sky.* That's how you do it. All you have to do is give and practice this divine love.

—*Wayne Dyer*

Wealth is a tool that gives you choices, but it can't compensate for a life not fully lived.

—*Oprah*

CHAPTER NINE

THE REWARD

My father, Vernon Winfrey, graduated from Hasla Barber College in 1963.

After working a year and a half as an apprentice, he opened his own barber shop in Nashville, where he's been a local fixture for the past fifty-three years. Before entering the barber college, he served in the army and held several other jobs, including as a janitor at Vanderbilt University. Both my mother, Vernita, and grandmother, Hattie Mae, were housekeepers.

I was raised knowing the value of a hard day's work. And from an early age, I have always known I was responsible for myself. Where I came from, there was no backup plan or safety net. For better or worse, you made your own way.

My first job was at fifteen, as a babysitter making fifty cents an hour. The children were a hand-ful, and the lady of the house always made sure to leave a big pile of clothes in her bedroom for me to clean up. Like clockwork, just before she left, she would turn to me and ask if I would mind "tidying things up." When she came home—and neglected to give me anything extra for cleaning—I understood very well that this woman didn't value my efforts. But I did. I valued my work and myself, and I decided that no matter how much or how little money I made, I would never let that define my worth. That babysitting job taught me my first valuable lesson about money: *I am not my salary*.

I gave up babysitting and moved on to stocking shelves in a local store for $1.50 an hour. The pay was better, but I was not allowed to speak to the customers. As I mentioned in chapter 4, I was known as the "talking child," so this was clearly not a good fit. I knew having a job where I had to stay silent was no way to earn a paycheck. It felt like a betrayal of myself. And even at fifteen, I was not willing to do that. The experience turned out to be another life lesson: *Sometimes knowing what you don't want is as valuable as knowing what you do.*

Eventually I moved on to work for my father, in a corner grocery store connected to his barbershop. I worked behind the counter selling penny candy. He didn't pay me, but I was allowed to talk. You could even say that the camaraderie in the barbershop and store explains why, years later, it felt so natural to be among the *Oprah Show* audience, listening to stories.

I was still in high school when I was offered a job as a newsreader at the local radio station. They paid me $100 a week. That was a lot of money for a seventeen-year-old, but I would have done it for free. It felt like the perfect fit. Lesson number three: *Know the joy of doing what you love and never stop pursuing it.*

All these years later, I am still keenly aware that I am not my salary. I give thanks every day for having the opportunity not only to make a living but to create what I see as an exquisite life. And I know that everyone needs a source of income in order to survive. But I have come to believe that one of the reasons I've enjoyed financial success is because my focus has never been on money.

As you experience the words of wisdom on the following pages, my hope is that you will begin to develop a new measure for true success. For me, the great reward is the feeling of lasting contentment and self-respect that comes when you are living out the truth of who you are.

One of the most memorable examples of the dangers of allowing material achievement to dictate self-worth is the story of author Sarah Ban Breathnach. I've said for years that Sarah's best-selling book *Simple Abundance* is the reason I started keeping a gratitude journal; it changed the way I moved through the world. *Simple Abundance* sold seven million copies, and before she knew it, Sarah was a multimillionaire. As a bonafide publishing superstar, she hired nine assistants, brought home eight pairs of Manolo Blahnik shoes in one trip, and bought the actual chapel once owned by Sir Isaac Newton. But fifteen years later Sarah joined me for a moving conversation in which she courageously shared the story of how she lost it all— and what she eventually gained in return.

What I learned from Sarah and so many others is that the way people handle money reflects the way they see themselves. Many times when people win the lottery and experience a windfall, they don't see themselves as worthy of their newfound riches. They wind up spending on possessions to create an idea of self-worth. When you've become blinded by the status symbols, it's easy to lose sight of the unique gifts only you can offer the world.

What I know for sure is that no matter how much wealth you come to possess, everything passes and changes with time. What is real, what is forever, is who you are and what you are meant to share with the world.

That is your true treasure.

—Oprah

I think luxury is a matter not of all
the things you have, but of all the
things you can afford to do without.

—*Pico Iyer*

CICELY TYSON

When I read a script, either my skin tingles, or my stomach churns. It's that simple. If my skin tingles I know it's something I must do. If my stomach churns I know it is something I cannot do. I have learned something from every single character that I've played. Something emotionally, spiritually, and psychologically true. I've never done a job just for money. I could not do anything that would not enhance humanity, especially for women.

It's so easy when the money is flashed before you to allow that to govern your choices. But it's more important to me to have peace of mind, body, and soul than to have all of the riches. When I put my head on my pillow at night I don't require a drug, alcohol, or anything else. Just fatigue.

MICHAEL BERNARD BECKWITH

MICHAEL BERNARD BECKWITH: Once you release your grasp, then you give up your resistance, and then that which is for you will come to you.

OPRAH: Aha. *That's the* aha *moment. Because when you want it, want it, want it, it doesn't show up.*

MICHAEL: Yes. Your message to the Universe at that moment is, *I want it I want it I want it I want it,* which is translating into, *I don't have it I don't have it I don't have it,* so you can't receive it.

OPRAH: *So you end up blocking your own blessing in that way.*

MICHAEL: Totally.

LYNNE TWIST

LYNNE TWIST: I've learned a great deal from the people I used to call poor and the people I used to call rich. And now I just realize we're all whole and complete people living in the ebb and flow of financial circumstances that change all the time and do not define us.

OPRAH: *I thought it was interesting how you say we question everything else. We question race, religion, other life circumstances. But money—we just give it the power.*

LYNNE: It's not that we have it. It has us. And we've assigned it more power than human life. More power than the natural world. More power than our relationships with each other. And we all know that's not true. But we live as if money's more important than anything else. And it cripples us. It gives us tremendous anxiety and suffering.

Somehow we drop this wonderful sense of value and worth and love and relationship that we have in the rest of life and we become irritable and competitive and greedy. There is so much suffering in this world in people's relationship with money. There's lying. There are things people wish they had never done. Things they didn't do that they wish they had done. You know, everybody has baggage.

OPRAH: *Because of the silent power of money. That's what you call it.*

LYNNE: Yes, we just think it will resolve everything. Everybody thinks, *Well, if I just had 30 percent more, everything would be fine.* But 30 percent ago, it wasn't fine. So 30 percent more won't really do it. Because when you get there, you want 30 percent more. We're just completely addicted in a society that values money above all else. And it's hurtful. It wounds us.

OPRAH: *So in order to break that scarcity myth, that belief that there's not enough, you say we need to live in the place of sufficiency.*

LYNNE: Yes. Sufficiency is a place of wholeness and completeness and deep understanding of who we are. And it's almost impossible to get to enough-ness or sufficiencies in a world that exalts what I call the "myth of scarcity"—which is a mind-set, an unconscious, unexamined set of assumptions of "not enough." There's not enough time. There's not enough money. There's not enough love. There are not enough vacations. There's not enough sex. There's not enough this. There's not enough that. And every meeting, every conversation, every lunch, every dinner, every everything is about what we don't have enough of. It's the siren song of a consumer culture. It's not just

about money. It dribbles over into every aspect of life.

OPRAH: *Everything.*

LYNNE: Yes. It's not just there is not enough, it's not enough. We're not enough. I'm not enough. And that deficit relationship with ourselves is the source of so much of our suffering. It comes from this unconscious, unexamined mind-set I call "scarcity," which has made up these myths. There is not enough to go around. And someone somewhere is always going to be left out.

OPRAH: *And if you believe that, and buy into that, then that's exactly what you will create.*

LYNNE: Exactly. It gives people permission to accumulate way more than they need out of the fear that they're not going to have enough. So even massive accumulation often comes from the fear *I'm not going to have enough for me.*

SARAH BAN BREATHNACH

SARAH BAN BREATHNACH: *Simple Abundance* was number one for almost a year. It was on the best-seller list for 119 weeks. And I've never shared this before because you don't get much sympathy for this part of the story; the Wednesday that there was no call from the publisher, I thought, *Oh, that's sort of strange. No one called.* So I called my agent and I said, "I haven't heard anything." She said, "Well, you're not on the best-seller list this week."

OPRAH: *How was that after 119 weeks?*

SARAH: I cried and cried. I thought no one in the world would understand what this feels like. The only trouble with being number one is eventually you have to be number two, three, and four.

OPRAH: *Because life moves on.*

SARAH: It does. It does.

OPRAH: *But hadn't you prepared yourself and said,* Well, what's going to happen when that call doesn't come?

SARAH: I didn't. That's one of the lessons I wish I had realized. I wish I had learned that success goes in cycles.

OPRAH: *But this is the thing, Sarah. This is the thing. What I feel strongly is that not only is it cyclical, but you've also got to understand that when you're in the midst of a phenomenon, you weren't looking for a hit.*

SARAH: Right. I wasn't looking for a best-selling book.

OPRAH: *You were looking for a way to speak to the hearts of women. That's what you were looking to do. Am I correct?*

SARAH: I was. You know, the only woman whose life I was trying to change when I was writing *Simple Abundance* was my own. And then the miracle was that it was just touching other women's lives.

JACK CANFIELD

I think the greatest wound we've all experienced is somehow being rejected for being our authentic self. And as a result of that, we then try to be what we're not to get approval, love, protection, safety, money, whatever. And the real need for all of us is to reconnect with the essence of who we really are and reown all the disowned parts of ourselves, whether it's our emotions, our spirituality, whatever. We all go around hiding parts of ourselves.

I was with a Buddhist teacher a number of years ago. And he said, "Let me give you the secret. If you were to meditate for twenty years, this is where you'd finally get to: *Just be yourself. But be all of you.*"

GOLDIE HAWN

It's a great thing to be recognized for something that you've done. But it's a moment in time. You can't live off of those accolades and make them the sum total of your importance in life, or your purpose in life. You can't let them define who you are. Those awards, they're wonderful. But they're never going to define you. I define myself by my ability to give. I define myself by my ability to understand. I define myself by my ethics and by my truth. These are the things that inform who I am, other than exterior moments that ebb and flow.

JORDAN PEELE

OPRAH: *I remember reading an article, as I was ending my show, and it was an article about Michael Jackson. His friends were commenting, saying he did* Thriller *and then spent the rest of his life chasing* Thriller. *And even though he sold twenty million albums from* Bad, *or forty million, whatever the number was, he was comparing everything in his life, still, to the end, to* Thriller. *So how do you now avoid the trap because* Get Out, *your first film, first directing, first written, has become this phenomenon?*

JORDAN PEELE: You know, I will continue to make movies—the movies that I want to see. If I want to see it, I have to have trust that other people will. And if they don't, I have to accept that's what it is. But for me, the biggest reward of all of this has always been the fact that I get to make another movie.

JIMMY KIMMEL

I've been at a major crossroads on a number of occasions. I was working at a radio station in Los Angeles and was making a decent amount of money. Then I was offered a lot more money by another radio station to compete against the guys that I worked with. I went to my boss and said, "Hey, listen, I'm being offered all this money to go against you guys." And he said, "Well, we can't pay you that much money." I thought about it. And I decided that even though it was a life-changing amount of money for me, I would not do it. I would just not feel right about competing against people that I liked, who were my friends and teammates. It wasn't three months later that I got a TV show.

JEFF WEINER

Failure is what is going to humble you. It helps you realize how fleeting success can be—at least traditional measures of success. You realize, to some extent, how beyond your control it is. And you invest less in it in terms of the way you define yourself. Success in terms of achieving objectives, in terms of manifesting a mission, in terms of manifesting a vision, that's all good, especially if what you do can create good in the world. But to the extent that you start to define yourself through traditional measures of success—to the extent that that's your source of self-esteem, you are destined to be unhappy because you cannot control it.

TREVOR NOAH

TREVOR NOAH: You've been to Soweto. You've seen how we live there.

OPRAH: *Yes.*

TREVOR: The weird thing is, I always say to people, "When you're poor, being poor sucks. But being poor together makes it a lot better." Right? Because you're in it together. And it doesn't discount the fact that you don't have much. But then you start to enjoy the things that you do have. And that is each other. And so we laughed. We enjoyed ourselves. We had something that sometimes you don't have when you have too much. And that is the ability to focus on the human beings around you.

WILLIAM PAUL YOUNG

OPRAH: *We live in this world where we're just all looking for more and more and more. We're looking for more things to fill us up and more things to make us whole. But you say the opposite of more is enough.*

WILLIAM PAUL YOUNG: Yes. And that really came to fruition in dealing with the loss of everything financial in my life.

OPRAH: *You lost everything because of what, business investments?*

PAUL: Yeah. And stupidity back in the day. So, I have all these men

friends in my life who have really brought healing to my soul. Right? So I call 'em up and I say, "Look, I know you love us. Here's our financial situation. I know you love my family. You're guys. You like to fix things. Please. Please. Don't rescue me from this. Because you're probably going to be interfering with what God is doing in my heart."

OPRAH: *So you let yourself fall?*

PAUL: I allowed myself to fall into trust. And that's when we learned that the opposite of more is enough.

OPRAH: *Most people would have said, "Could you loan me the money? I promise this won't happen again if you only would help me."*

PAUL: I know.

OPRAH: *That is so profound. Because I'm the person who a lot of people come to and ask, "Could you help me out? If you could only do this." And what I have learned is, money never saves people.*

PAUL: You're absolutely right.

OPRAH: *It only delays whatever was already waiting for you. Because you* have created the situation based upon the way you've handled or managed your life. That's why what you just said is such a big aha revelation. By writing the check, I have blocked people from receiving whatever lessons they needed to learn.

PAUL: Right. Because they think that money will give them the control that will conquer their fear.

OPRAH: *Oh, my God. That is so profound for me.*

PAUL: And it was profound for us. Suddenly joy dropped on us like a ton of bricks. And we had nothing.

You already know.

—*Oprah*

CHAPTER TEN

HOME

Throughout my life (and I bet yours, too), certain works of literature and film have completely changed the lens through which I see the world.

This list is long for me, but there are two classics in particular that I treasure.

I was in my early years of high school, living with my mother in Milwaukee, when a librarian made a recommendation that would change me forever. She noticed that I checked out five books each visit, and said, "If you like reading these kinds of books, you might like *To Kill a Mockingbird*."

She was right.

The moment I picked it up, I was entranced. The story of Boo Radley, Scout, and Atticus Finch is probably the reason I started a book club—because it was one of the first books that I wanted *everyone* around me to read. I was drawn to Scout's spirit. I felt a kinship with her curiosity and admired that despite her age, young Scout knew exactly who she was and what she believed. I felt emboldened by Scout. At the time, I was awakening to the idea of racism, just like her. And her eyes were opening to the complex realities of the world, just like mine.

I also wanted the kind of relationship Scout had with her father, Atticus, especially when she called him by his first name. Many years after I'd read the book, I found myself at a luncheon seated next to Gregory Peck, who portrayed Atticus in the movie version of the book. The only words I could think to say were, "So, how's Scout?" Mr. Peck was gracious and answered my question about his costar who played the little girl. "Well," he said, "that was forty years ago, so she's okay."

To me, Scout was as powerful a character that day as she was the first time I opened the book and then saw her come to life in the movie. A part of Scout will reside in me for the rest of my life.

It was the plight of another strong-willed girl, in one of the most beloved films of all time, that unlocked an early spiritual awakening for me.

I was seven or eight years old when I figured out that *The Wizard of Oz* was more than a story about a bump on the head and a fantastical dream. The moment I realized that the Scarecrow, the Tin Man, and the Cowardly Lion were actually Dorothy's friends from Auntie Em's farm, something clicked deep within.

I didn't have the words to express it at the time, but as I grew into my own path of awareness, I understood *The Wizard of Oz* to be one of the great spiritual teachings of all time. Dorothy was on what the great philosopher Joseph Campbell so famously called "a hero's journey." The Yellow Brick Road represented

the path toward her true self. Along the way, she encountered the disempowered parts of herself—the Scarecrow's wish for a brain, the Tin Man's desire for a heart, and the Cowardly Lion's longing for courage.

Like so many of us, Dorothy believed she needed something outside herself—in her case, the Great and Powerful Oz—to bestow the cherished virtues on her friends and bring her home.

But, in what I believe is the most powerful moment of the film, Glinda the Good Witch says the words that spiritual teachers have been trying to convey for thousands of years.

"You don't need to be helped any longer," Glinda tells Dorothy. "You've always had the power."

Dorothy's most trusted companion, the Scarecrow, asks Glinda, "Then why didn't you tell her before?"

And Glinda replies, "Because she wouldn't have believed me. She had to learn it for herself."

This was probably the greatest *aha* moment of my life.

No matter how far away from yourself you may have strayed, there is always a path back. You already know who you are and how to fulfill your destiny. And your ruby slippers are ready to carry you home.

Just before Dorothy clicks her heels, she shares the universal lesson that applies to each and every person here on earth: "If I ever go looking for my heart's desire again, I won't look any further than my own backyard. Because if it isn't there, I never really lost it to begin with."

The final chapter of this book is meant to illustrate that you have the power to discover your purpose and live your greatest truth. It doesn't matter how many yellow brick roads you encounter—it has always been right there, at home, in your heart.

—*Oprah*

We are all created with this phenomenal force inside of us. And everything that comes our way, is coming our way so that we can grow and evolve. And if we look at it like that, if we're willing to open our hearts and see where we're shut down, where we're trying to resist life, then we have the great opportunity to step into who we always wanted to be.

—*Debbie Ford*

Father RICHARD ROHR

All spiritual knowledge is not cognition. It's recognition. You're reknowing what you deeply already knew. What you deeply intuited, suspected, desired, hoped for, that's the soul. The discovery of yourself and the discovery of God will eventually be parallel movements. You fall deeper into yourself. You fall deeper into God. You fall deeper into God, you have permission to fall deeper into yourself.

SUE MONK KIDD

I have this phrase I use: *the old woman*. I say that with great fondness. My daughter and I once went on travels. On those journeys, I was searching for that old woman. The woman I wanted to grow into. She's wise. She's bold. She's strong and resilient. She knows her voice, she speaks it, and she stands by it. This is the old woman for me. She's distilled down. In my novel *The Invention of Wings*, there's a moment at the end where Handful looks at Sarah and says she's been boiled down into a good strong broth. I want to be that. I want to be a good strong broth that has those qualities of the old woman I went off searching for.

ELIZABETH GILBERT

OPRAH: *What did you discover that you never knew you had?*

ELIZABETH GILBERT: I discovered I could take care of myself completely. I've got my own back. And I don't just mean financially. I mean emotionally. I know that I became a responsible enough adult to be allowed to be alone with the child who is inside of me.

OPRAH: *And you know that no matter what, you're going to be all right.*

ELIZABETH: I'm going to be all right.

ELIZABETH LESSER

OPRAH: *I know the lesson you wish for all of us is to live each day from the marrow.*

ELIZABETH LESSER: Yes. We think that the answer to life is compli-cated or you've got to go on some big quest to find out who you are. But it turns out that deep inside you are already enough, just because you are.

STEVIE NICKS

My life is a testament to believing that if you want something, you can make it happen. So hope springs eternal. Yes, you will take another beautiful picture. Yes, you will walk onstage in a long black skinny dress again. It's possible. So I think what you just have to tell people is, "It's all possible."

SIDNEY POITIER

I am most proud of being accepted as a useful human being. Useful to my children, to my parents, who are no longer here, to my friends, to my environment. I am not the human being that I would one day hope to be, but I have come a long way. I really have come a very long way. And I'm proud of that, because I am indeed a better person than once I ever was. We are imperfect creatures. We are, that's what it is. But we should try reaching for the better you, the better me. There is pain and there is difficulty, and there is fear and all the kinds of things that we live with. But it is through them we have to reach. We have to reach out, not just to each other, but to the Universe.

JACK CANFIELD

My belief is that the whole purpose of life is to gain mastery, mastery of our emotions, our finances, our relationships, our consciousness through meditation, things like that. And it's not about the stuff we achieve or amass in life. All the stuff can be taken away. People lose their fortunes. They lose their reputation. Beautiful spouses can die or leave you. But the mastery you achieve and who you became in the process of achieving those things can never be taken away. Never.

MITCH ALBOM

Morrie said the reason people were unhappy was because they walked through their lives like they were sleepwalking. They were following orders about what they should do with their life based on our culture. They weren't finding the meaning in their life through giving to other people, being involved with their community, or finding something creative, an outlet for themselves. They were busy trying to be somebody else's version of what they thought they should be. He ended up describing not only me, but an awful lot of people that I knew at that time. And I think he's right. And then, we get to the end and we're like, *Whoa, that can't be it.*

ELLEN DEGENERES

I'm in a relationship now where I have equal love. I love her and she loves me. We respect each other. We're kind and gentle to each other. And, as someone once said, it's wonderful to be loved, but it's profound to be understood.

SHAWN ACHOR

OPRAH: *You all have heard this question, "Is the glass half-empty or is the glass half-full?" I beat myself up because some days I look at it and I say,* It's definitely half-empty. *And some days,* It's half-full. *But what you're saying is, what does it matter if you have a pitcher nearby? I love this. So it doesn't matter if the glass is half-full or half-empty.*

SHAWN ACHOR: That's right. We get so focused on the glass, whether it's half-full or half-empty, and we can argue forever between optimists and pessimists. Both can say the other is being unrealistic. But

it wouldn't matter if we looked at more of the world and saw that there's a pitcher of water that's sitting next to it.

OPRAH: *Life is the pitcher.*

SHAWN: Life is the pitcher and we're missing the pitcher when we're so focused on that one element. It doesn't matter if your glass is half-full or half-empty if there's a pitcher of water right next to you. And we need to look at the full picture to see the full pitcher.

Optimism is like a muscle that gets stronger with use. When you want to build a muscle, you've got to keep using it. That's how you have to be. I'm an eternal optimist and so I can find those little silver linings, those little moral victories. It takes courage to believe that the best is yet to come.

—*Robin Roberts*

JEAN HOUSTON

I believe that we are here with deep purpose to become all that we can be. I believe that we are headed ultimately in the right direction. I believe that we have been given sufficient stress, crisis, complexity, and consciousness to do things that are just beyond our imagination. Larger than our aspiration. More complex than all our dreams. I believe in love. I believe in you. I believe in me. I believe in this, the most potent moment in human history.

———————

JANE FONDA

I've done a lot of things in my life. There are a lot of parts to my life. I have thought very deliberately and intentionally about my life, and why certain things happen and what they mean. I learned that the goal is to be whole. To reside inside your skin. I don't want to die tomorrow, but if I do, I'd go out happy. Because I've worked hard at making the most of what I've been given. And the lesson is: It's never too late.

GARY ZUKAV

OPRAH: *It's just like the moment when the Wicked Witch of the West is trying to get to Dorothy. And Glinda says, "Oh, rubbish! You have no power here. Be gone ..." The goodness and the light is so strong that the Wicked Witch of the West has no ability to affect that territory.*

GARY ZUKAV: That's right. The Universe doesn't look in terms of good, bad, better, worse, success, or failure. It looks in terms of limitation and opportunity. The more the loving parts of your personality are the ones you're cultivating, the more opportunity you have. The more fear is controlling you, the more limitation you have. Because what is failure? We can't possibly know what failure is. We cannot.

OPRAH: *Some people think they do.*

GARY: Most people think they do. But that's because they're judging how they feel their lives should be and what they need to be. A success. Who is to say what's a success or what's a failure? Do your best. Trust. Relax. Enjoy yourself.

*Nourish what makes you feel
confident, connected, contented.
Opportunity will rise to meet you.*

—*Oprah*

EPILOGUE

Some of the most meaningful experiences on *The Oprah Winfrey Show* happened when it was perfectly still, just a single person on the stage sharing a story so intimate you had to hold your breath just to hear it.

Years ago, I interviewed a grieving mother whose adult son had died after a long illness. You could have heard a pin drop in the studio when she so beautifully told the story of their final moment together. The mother had climbed into bed with her son. She could barely hear him, but her head was on his chest. As he took his last breath, he whispered, "Oh Mom, it is all so simple. It's so simple, Mom." He then closed his eyes and died.

I got chills when I heard that. I realized then, just as it resonates with me now: We allow life to get so complicated—when it's really so very simple.

From that day forward I resolved to continually ask myself, *How am I making things more difficult than they need to be?*

Your answer to that same question is the next step in your path. It's that simple.

Imagine what lies just around the bend.

Can you see it? I can.

Love,
Oprah

CONTRIBUTORS

SHAWN ACHOR, p. 184: Shawn Achor is a Harvard University happiness researcher, author, and speaker. He is the *New York Times* best-selling author of *Before Happiness* and *The Happiness Advantage*. In 2007, Shawn founded GoodThink Inc. and later cofounded the Institute for Applied Positive Research with his wife, Michelle Gielan. Shawn's most recent work is *Big Potential: How Transforming the Pursuit of Success Raises Our Achievement, Happiness, and Well-Being*.

ADYASHANTI, p. 52: Adyashanti is a spiritual teacher and author who offers talks, online courses, and retreats in the United States and abroad. Together with his wife, Mukti, he is the founder of Open Gate Sangha Inc., a nonprofit organization that supports and makes available his teachings. Adyashanti's best-selling books include *The Way of Liberation, Resurrecting Jesus, Falling into Grace*, and *The End of Your World*.

MITCH ALBOM, pp. 70, 183: Mitch Albom is a best-selling author, journalist, screenwriter, playwright, and broadcaster. Collectively, his books have sold more than thirty-five million copies worldwide, have been published in forty-five languages around the world, and have been made into Emmy Award–winning and critically acclaimed television movies.

INDIA.ARIE, pp. 74–75: India.Arie is a four-time Grammy Award–winning singer, songwriter, actress, and musician. She has sold ten million albums worldwide.

REVEREND ED BACON, p. 36: Ed Bacon is an Episcopal priest and author of *8 Habits of Love: Overcome Fear and Transform Your Life*. For twenty-one years he was the senior priest of the largest Episcopal congregation in the western United States, All Saints Church, located in Los Angeles. He is a vocal advocate for LGBTQ justice and marriage as well as dismantling all forms of systemic bigotry. A leader in interfaith circles, he teaches how our Oneness in Love overcomes our separateness in fear. He also works to help save the Pando forest in southern Utah, the largest organism on the planet, which he considers symbolic of the interconnectedness of all creation.

SARAH BAN BREATHNACH, pp. 162–163: Sarah Ban Breathnach is a best-selling author, philanthropist, and public speaker. She is the author of thirteen books, including *Simple Abundance: A Daybook of Comfort and Joy*, which sold more than five million copies and spent more than two years on the *New York Times* best-seller list, and *Peace and Plenty: Finding Your Path to Financial Serenity*. Her forthcoming book is a completely revised and updated

Simple Abundance: A 21st Century Guide to Comfort and Contentment.

MICHAEL BERNARD BECKWITH, pp. 76, 98, 159: Michael Bernard Beckwith is the founder and spiritual director of the Agape International Spiritual Center, a trans-denominational community of thousands. Michael is a sought-after meditation teacher, speaker, and seminar leader whose many books focus on the transformative Life Visioning Process, which he originated. He is the author of several top-selling books, including *Spiritual Liberation: Fulfilling Your Soul's Potential* and *Life Visioning: A Transformative Process for Activating Your Unique Gifts and Highest Potential.*

ROB BELL, p. 126: Rob Bell is the *New York Times* best-selling author of *Love Wins, What We Talk About When We Talk About God, The Zimzum of Love* (cowritten with his wife, Kristen), and his most recent book, *What Is the Bible?* He hosts the podcast *The RobCast,* and in 2014 was a featured speaker on Oprah's Life You Want Tour.

NATE BERKUS, p. 30: Nate Berkus first established his award-winning interior design firm at the age of twenty-four. Since then, his approachable and elevated design philosophy has transformed countless spaces around the world. He has produced a number of successful home collections and television shows and is a *New York Times* best-selling author.

PASTOR A. R. BERNARD, p. 20: A. R. Bernard is the founder, senior pastor, and CEO of the over 45,000-member Christian Cultural Center located in Brooklyn, New York. He served as the president of the Council of Churches of the City of New York, representing 1.5 million Protestants, Anglicans, and Orthodox Christians. He served on the NYC Economic Development Corporation Board and on NYC School Chancellor's Advisory Cabinet. Pastor Bernard is also the author of two books, including his most recent work, *Four Things Women Want from a Man.*

GABRIELLE BERNSTEIN, p. 88: Gabrielle Bernstein is an international speaker and author of the number one *New York Times* best-seller *The Universe Has Your Back: Transform Fear to Faith* and six additional best-selling books. Gabrielle has been called a "next-generation thought leader." In September 2019, she releases her seventh book, *Super Attractor.*

VICE PRESIDENT JOE BIDEN, pp. 39, 94, 124: Joe Biden represented Delaware for thirty-six years in the U.S. Senate before serving as forty-seventh vice president of the United States from 2009 to 2017. Since leaving the White House, he created the Biden Foundation, the Penn Biden Center for Diplomacy & Global Engagement at the University of Pennsylvania, and the Biden Institute at the University of Delaware. He is the author of *Promises to Keep: On Life and Politics* and the number one *New York Times* best-seller, *Promise Me, Dad: A Year of Hope, Hardship, and Purpose.*

JON BON JOVI, p. 132: Jon Bon Jovi is a singer-songwriter, musician, philanthropist, actor, father of four, and husband. To date, his Grammy Award–winning band, Bon Jovi, has sold more than 130 million albums worldwide and was inducted into the Rock & Roll Hall of Fame in 2018. The socially conscious artist founded The Jon Bon Jovi Soul Foundation in 2006, to combat issues that force families and individuals into economic despair.

DAVID BROOKS, p. 93: David Brooks is an op-ed columnist for *The New York Times* and appears regularly on *PBS NewsHour* and *Meet the Press.* He is the best-selling author of *The Road to Character*; *The Social Animal: The Hidden Sources of Love, Character, and Achievement*; *Bobos in Paradise: The New Upper Class and How They Got There*; and *On Paradise Drive: How We Live Now (And Always Have) in the Future Tense.*

BRENÉ BROWN, pp. 90–91: Dr. Brené Brown is a research professor at the University of Houston, where she holds the Huffington Brené Brown Endowed Chair at the Graduate College of Social Work. She has spent the past two decades studying courage, vulnerability, shame, and empathy and is the author of four number one *New York Times* best-sellers: *The Gifts of Imperfection, Daring Greatly,*

Rising Strong, and *Braving the Wilderness.* Her latest book, *Dare to Lead,* was released in October 2018. Brené's TED Talk—"The Power of Vulnerability"—is one of the top five most-viewed TED Talks in the world with over 35 million views.

JACK CANFIELD, pp. 164, 182: Jack Canfield is the coauthor of the beloved *Chicken Soup for the Soul*® series. He has taught millions his formulas for success and now certifies trainers to teach his content and methodology all over the world. Jack is the author and coauthor of more than 150 books, including the best-selling *The Success Principles™: How to Get from Where You Are to Where You Want to Be.*

PRESIDENT JIMMY CARTER, p. 147: Jimmy Carter served as the thirty-ninth president of the United States from 1977 to 1981. In 1982, he became a University Distinguished Professor at Emory University in Atlanta, Georgia, and founded the Carter Center, which focuses on resolving conflict, promoting democracy, protecting human rights, and preventing disease worldwide. President Carter was awarded the 2002 Nobel Peace Prize and is the author of twenty-nine books, including his most recent, *A Full Life: Reflections at Ninety.*

RUPAUL CHARLES, p. 37: RuPaul Charles is an actor, model, singer-songwriter, television personality, and author. He is considered to be the most commercially successful drag queen in the United States. Since 2009, RuPaul has produced and hosted the reality competition series *RuPaul's Drag Race*, for which he received four Primetime Emmy Awards. He has published two books and released fourteen studio albums to date, including *Glamazon* (2011), *Born Naked* (2014), and *American* (2017).

SISTER JOAN CHITTISTER, pp. 34– 35: For forty years, Sister Joan Chittister has passionately advocated on behalf of peace, human rights, women's issues, and church renewal. A Benedictine sister, Sister Joan is an international lecturer, counselor, and best-selling author of more than sixty books, including award-winning *The Gift of Years*. She writes an online column for the *National Catholic Reporter* and a blog for *HuffPost*. Sister Joan currently serves as cochair of the Global Peace Initiative of Women, a partner organization of the U.N.

PEMA CHÖDRÖN, p. 55: Pema Chödrön is a Buddhist teacher, nun, author, mother, and grandmother. She is widely known for her down-to-earth interpretation of Tibetan Buddhism for Western audiences. She has written several books, including her most recent, *Fail, Fail Again, Fail Better: Wise Advice for Leaning into the Unknown*, and the *New York Times* best-seller *When Things Fall Apart*.

DEEPAK CHOPRA, MD, FACP, pp. 25, 108, 143: A world-renowned pioneer in integrative medicine and personal transformation, Deepak Chopra is the founder of the Chopra Foundation and cofounder of Jiyo.com and the Chopra Center for Wellbeing. He is the author of more than eighty-six books, including numerous *New York Times* best-sellers. His most recent book is *The Healing Self: A Revolutionary New Plan to Supercharge Your Immunity and Stay Well for Life*.

STEPHEN COLBERT, pp. 92, 123: Stephen Colbert currently hosts the Emmy-nominated late-night talk show *The Late Show with Stephen Colbert*. From 2005 to 2014, he hosted *The Colbert Report* on Comedy Central, following his eight years as a correspondent on *The Daily Show*. *The Report* received two Peabody Awards, two Grammy Awards, seven Emmy Awards, and thirty-seven total Emmy nominations. Stephen is the author of four books, including his most recent work, *Stephen Colbert's Midnight Confessions*.

CINDY CRAWFORD, p. 132: Cindy Crawford has graced over one thousand magazine covers worldwide, including *Vogue, Elle, W, Harper's Bazaar, Cosmopolitan,* and *Allure*. In 2005, Cindy created a line of beauty products with Jean-Louis Sebagh called Meaningful Beauty for Guthy-Renker. *Becoming*, a book about Cindy's life and career cowritten with Katherine O'Leary, was published in September 2015 and is a *New York Times* best-seller.

ELLEN DEGENERES, pp. 32, 183:
Ellen is a comedian, television host, actress, writer, producer, and LGBT activist. She starred in the sitcom *Ellen* from 1994 to 1998 and has hosted *The Ellen DeGeneres Show* since 2003. Ellen has hosted the Academy Awards, the Grammy Awards, and the Primetime Emmys. She has authored four books and started her own record company, Eleveneleven, as well as a production company, A Very Good Production. She also launched a lifestyle brand, ED Ellen DeGeneres. Ellen has won thirty Emmys, twenty People's Choice Awards, and numerous other awards for her work and charitable efforts. In 2016, she received the Presidential Medal of Freedom.

GLENNON DOYLE, pp. 38, 130: Glennon Doyle is the author of the number one *New York Times* best-seller and Oprah's Book Club selection *Love Warrior*, as well as the *New York Times* best-seller *Carry On, Warrior*. Glennon is a nationally recognized public speaker and the founder of the popular blog *Momastery*. She is the founder and president of Together Rising, a nonprofit organization that turns collective heartbreak into collective action by raising and deploying more than $14 million for people in crisis.

WAYNE DYER, p. 150: Wayne Dyer's first book, *Your Erroneous Zones*, is one of the best-selling books of all time, with an estimated thirty-five million copies sold to date. Over the four decades of his career,

he wrote more than forty books, including twenty-one *New York Times* best-sellers. Prior to his death in 2015, Wayne had expanded his message through lecture tours, a series of audiotapes, PBS programs, and regular publication of new books.

CHARLES EISENSTEIN, pp. 144–145:
Charles Eisenstein is a speaker and writer focusing on themes of civilization, consciousness, money, and human cultural evolution. His viral short films and essays online have established him as a social philosopher and countercultural intellectual. He is the author of several books, including *The Ascent of Humanity*, *Sacred Economics*, and *The More Beautiful World Our Hearts Know Is Possible*.

JANE FONDA, p. 186: Jane Fonda is a two-time Academy Award–winning actress, producer, author, activist, and fitness guru. Her career has spanned over fifty years, including over forty-five films and crucial work on behalf of political causes, women's rights, Native Americans, and the environment. As a three-time Golden Globe winner and 2014 recipient of the AFI Life Achievement Award, Jane continues her career by currently starring in Netflix's hit series *Grace & Frankie* for which she received an Emmy nomination for Outstanding Lead Actress in a Comedy Series in 2017. *Jane Fonda in Five Acts*, a documentary chronicling Jane's life and her activism, premiered in 2018 on HBO. Jane celebrated her eightieth birthday by raising $1 million for each of her nonprofits, Georgia Campaign for Adolescent Power & Potential and The Women's Media Center.

DEBBIE FORD, pp. 77, 177: Prior to her death in 2013, Debbie Ford was an internationally recognized expert in the field of personal transformation and a pioneering force in incorporating the study and integration of the human shadow into modern psychological and spiritual practices. She was the *New York Times* best-selling author of ten books, including *The Dark Side of the Light Chasers*, *Spiritual Divorce*, *Why Good People Do Bad Things*, and *The 21-Day Consciousness Cleanse*.

DEVON FRANKLIN, p. 99: DeVon Franklin is an award-winning film and TV producer, best-selling author, renowned preacher and spiritual success coach. DeVon serves as president/CEO of Franklin Entertainment. As a filmmaker, DeVon is producing the inspirational true story *Breakthrough* starring Chrissy Metz in theaters Easter of 2019. Along with his work as a producer, DeVon is the author of *The Truth About Men*, *The Hollywood Commandments*, *New York Times* best-seller *The Wait* (cowritten with his wife, award-winning actress Meagan Good), and *Produced By Faith*.

ELIZABETH GILBERT, pp. 22, 80, 179: Elizabeth Gilbert's 2006 memoir, *Eat Pray Love*, sparked a global conversation about

what it means to fulfill your life's purpose. The book was an international best-seller, translated into over thirty languages, with over ten million copies sold worldwide. Elizabeth has since written several other best-sellers, including her most recent, *Big Magic: Creative Living Beyond Fear*. Elizabeth is a highly sought-after public speaker, sharing her personal story and insight on personal growth and happiness.

MEAGAN GOOD, p. 99: Meagan Good is one of Hollywood's most sought-after leading ladies, a producer, and the *New York Times* best-selling author of *The Wait*. She is currently making her directorial debut and starring in the indie feature *If Not Now, When*. She just wrapped the feature film *Motivated Seller* and Lee Daniels' *Star* on Fox. Good is the executive producer of *A Boy. A Girl. A Dream: Love On Election Night*, which debuted at the 2018 Sundance Film Festival. And as the cofounder of the non-profit The Greater Good Foundation, she continues to prove that young women can do and be anything they choose.

BRIAN GRAZER, p. 31: Brian Grazer is an Oscar-, Emmy-, Golden Globe- and Grammy-winning film and television producer. His films and TV series have been nominated for 43 Academy Awards and 195 Emmys. In 2002, Brian won the Best Picture Oscar for *A Beautiful Mind* and in 2015, he published his *New York Times* best-selling book *A Curious Mind: The Secret to a Bigger Life*, in which he discusses conversations with interesting people from all backgrounds, many of whom inspired his work.

GOLDIE HAWN, pp. 103, 165: Goldie Hawn is an Academy Award–winning actress, director, and producer. Her most recent film is 2017's *Snatched.* In 2003, Goldie founded the Hawn Foundation, a nonprofit organization that provides youth education programs intended to improve academic performance through "life-enhancing strategies for well-being."

JEAN HOUSTON, pp. 24, 186: Jean Houston, PhD, is a scholar, philosopher, and researcher in human capacities. She is noted for her ability to combine a deep knowledge of history, culture, new science, spirituality, and human development into her teaching. She is the author of thirty books and a past consultant for the United Nations and to international leaders and communities around the world.

PICO IYER, p. 157: Essayist, novelist, and world-renowned travel writer Pico Iyer was born in Oxford, England, to parents from India, raised in California, and educated at Eton, Oxford, and Harvard. Since 1987, he has been based in western Japan. Apart from the two novels and ten works of nonfiction he has published, he is also a highly sought-after speaker. Between 2013 and 2016, Pico delivered three TED Talks.

TRACEY JACKSON, p. 129: Tracey Jackson is an author, blogger, screenwriter, film director, and producer. One of her two best-selling books was written with Grammy-winning songwriter Paul Williams, titled *Gratitude & Trust: Six Affirmations That Will Change Your Life.* It combines the knowledge Paul gained in his twenty-four years of addiction recovery work with Tracey's lifelong quest for peace and a daily routine to get through life's challenges.

BISHOP T. D. JAKES, pp. 23, 46, 110: Bishop T. D. Jakes is the CEO of TDJ Enterprises and the founder and senior pastor of the Potter's House of Dallas, Inc., a global humanitarian organization and thirty-thousand-member church located in Dallas. His television show, *The Potter's Touch,* reaches sixty-seven million households per month, and his best-selling book *Woman, Thou Art Loosed!* became an award-winning feature film. He is the author of seven *New York Times* best-selling books. His latest work is *Soar!: Build Your Vision from the Ground Up.*

JAY-Z, p. 112: Shawn "Jay-Z" Carter is one of the best-selling musicians of all time, having sold more than fifty million albums and seventy-five million singles worldwide, while receiving twenty-one Grammy Awards for his music. Jay-Z is the former president of Def Jam Recordings, the cofounder of Roc-A-Fella Records, and the founder of the entertainment company

Roc Nation. He continues his philanthropic work through the Shawn Carter Foundation. Shawn Carter Scholars are studying at over one hundred institutions of higher learning throughout the nation.

JON KABAT-ZINN, p. 53: Jon Kabat-Zinn, PhD, is an internationally known scientist, writer, and meditation teacher. He is a professor of medicine emeritus at the University of Massachusetts Medical School, where he founded its world-renowned Mindfulness-Based Stress Reduction Clinic and the Center for Mindfulness in Medicine, Health Care, and Society. Jon is the author of several books, including the best-selling *Full Catastrophe Living: Using the Wisdom of Your Body and Mind to Face Stress, Pain, and Illness* and *Wherever You Go, There You Are: Mindfulness Meditation in Everyday Life.*

MINDY KALING, pp. 102, 148: Mindy Kaling is an actor, writer, director, and executive producer. She created, executive produced, and starred in the Hulu original comedy series *The Mindy Project* from 2012 to 2017. Prior to that, Mindy was known for her work on the critically acclaimed, Emmy Award–winning NBC show *The Office*. In addition to directing, producing, and portraying celebrity-obsessed Kelly Kapoor, Mindy wrote twenty-six episodes of the series. Mindy was the first woman of color nominated for an Emmy in writing. Mindy has also lent her voice to multiple blockbuster animated comedies including

the Oscar-winning Pixar film *Inside Out*. Her recent projects include Disney's *A Wrinkle in Time* and as a part of the star-studded cast of *Ocean's Eight*. She is the author of two *New York Times* best-sellers: *Is Everyone Hanging Out Without Me? (And Other Concerns)* and *Why Not Me?*

SUE MONK KIDD, pp. 18, 178: Sue Monk Kidd's first novel, *The Secret Life of Bees*, spent more than two and a half years on the *New York Times* best-seller list and later became a feature film. *The Invention of Wings* debuted on the *New York Times* best-seller list at number one and was chosen for Oprah's Book Club 2.0.

JIMMY KIMMEL, p. 167: Jimmy Kimmel serves as host and executive producer of the Emmy-winning late-night talk show *Jimmy Kimmel Live!* on ABC.

ELIZABETH LESSER, p. 180: Elizabeth Lesser is cofounder and senior adviser of Omega Institute, the largest adult education center in the United States focusing on health, wellness, spirituality, and creativity. Elizabeth is also the author of the *New York Times* best-selling book *Broken Open: How Difficult Times Can Help Us Grow*. Her latest work is *Marrow: Love, Loss, and What Matters Most.*

U.S. REPRESENTATIVE JOHN LEWIS, pp. 56, 141: During the height of the civil rights movement, from 1963 to 1966,

John Lewis was chairman of the Student Nonviolent Coordinating Committee (SNCC), which he helped form. On March 7, 1965, John Lewis and Hosea Williams led more than six hundred peaceful protesters advocating for voting rights across the Edmund Pettus Bridge in Selma, Alabama. News broadcasts and photographs revealing the senseless brutality of the state's response helped hasten the passage of the Voting Rights Act of 1965. He has served as U.S. representative of Georgia's Fifth Congressional District since 1986 where he is often called "the conscience of the U.S. Congress." He is one of the 2010 recipients of the Presidential Medal of Freedom and was also one of the ten speakers at the historic March on Washington.

TRACY MCMILLAN, p. 131: Tracy McMillan is best known for the 2011 viral blog post "Why You're Not Married," which for two years was the most-viewed article on the *Huffington Post*, and is the fourth most-read post of all time. She also wrote a book based on the piece, *Why You're Not Married ... Yet*. She is the author of a memoir, *I Love You and I'm Leaving You Anyway*, and the debut novel *You'll Know It When You See It*, published in 2015.

LIN-MANUEL MIRANDA, p. 32: Lin-Manuel Miranda is an award-winning composer, lyricist, playwright, and actor best known for creating and starring in the Broadway musicals *Hamilton* and *In the Heights*.

He cowrote the songs for Disney's *Moana* soundtrack. Lin-Manuel's awards include a Pulitzer Prize, three Grammy Awards, an Emmy Award, a MacArthur Fellowship, and three Tony Awards.

JANET MOCK, pp. 100–101: Janet Mock is a writer, director, and advocate. She is the *New York Times* best-selling author of two memoirs, *Redefining Realness* and *Surpassing Certainty*, as well as the host of the podcast series *Never Before with Janet Mock*. Janet is a multiplatform storyteller and is the first trans woman of color to write, produce, and direct a TV series with the critically acclaimed *Pose* on FX.

THOMAS MOORE, p. 59: Thomas Moore is the author of the best-selling book *Care of the Soul* and twenty-four other books on deepening spirituality and cultivating the soul. He has been a monk, a musician, a university professor, and a psychotherapist. Today he lectures widely on holistic medicine, spirituality, psychotherapy, and the arts. His most recent book is *Ageless Soul: The Lifelong Journey Toward Meaning and Joy*.

WES MOORE, p. 57: Wes Moore is a Rhodes scholar, army combat veteran, entrepreneur, and author of two *New York Times* best-selling books: *The Other Wes Moore* and *The Work*. He is also the CEO of Robin Hood, one of the largest poverty-fighting organizations in the country. He founded BridgeEdU with the hope of offering young scholars a better opportunity to succeed by reinventing the first-year college experience and building a better on-ramp to higher education and career preparedness.

TRACY MORGAN, p. 33: Tracy Morgan is an actor and comedian best known for his eight seasons as a cast member on *Saturday Night Live* and for his costarring role on the Emmy Award–winning television show *30 Rock*. Tracy currently stars in the TBS comedy *The Last O.G.*

ALANIS MORISSETTE, p. 127: With sales of over sixty million albums worldwide, Alanis Morissette has earned seven Grammy Awards, a Golden Globe nomination, and an induction into the Canadian Music Hall of Fame in 2015. She is also the host of the podcast *Conversation with Alanis Morissette.* As an activist, Alanis was awarded a U.N. Global Tolerance Award. She donates her time to help raise awareness and funding for Equality Now, Music for Relief, the *Every Mother Counts* CD, and P.S. Arts in California.

CAROLINE MYSS, pp. 25, 51, 72–73: Caroline Myss is a five-time *New York Times* best-selling author and internationally renowned speaker in the fields of human consciousness, spirituality and mysticism, health, energy medicine, and the science of medical intuition. Her seminal book, *Anatomy of the Spirit*, has sold more than 1.5 million copies. Her most recent work is *Archetypes: Who Are You?*

MARK NEPO, p. 138: Mark Nepo is a poet and philosopher who has taught for more than forty years in the fields of poetry, spirituality, and the journey of inner transformation. Mark is best known for his number-one *New York Times* best-seller *The Book of Awakening*. His most recent books are *More Together Than Alone*, *The Way Under the Way*, and *Things That Join the Sea and the Sky: Field Notes on Living.*

THICH NHAT HANH, p. 140: Zen master Thich Nhat Hanh is a global spiritual leader, poet, and peace activist, revered throughout the world for his powerful teachings and best-selling writings on mindfulness and peace. He has been a pioneer in bringing mindfulness to the West, founding eleven monasteries in America, Europe, and Asia, as well as more than one thousand local mindfulness practice communities. Thich Nhat Hanh has published more than one hundred titles on meditation, mindfulness, and engaged Buddhism, with some of the best-known books being *Peace Is Every Step*, *The Miracle of Mindfulness*, *Being Peace*, *Anger*, and *The Art of Power.*

STEVIE NICKS, p. 181: As a member of Fleetwood Mac and as a solo artist, Stevie Nicks has more than forty Top 50 hits and has sold more than 140 million records. She has garnered eight Grammy Award nominations and two American Music Award nominations as a solo artist. And she has received numerous awards and nominations with Fleetwood

Mac, including a Grammy Award and five Grammy Award nominations. Her charity foundation, titled Stevie Nicks' Band of Soldiers, is used for the benefit of wounded military personnel.

SHAUNA NIEQUIST, pp. 47–49: Shauna Niequist is the *New York Times* best-selling author of *Cold Tangerines, Bittersweet, Bread & Wine, Savor,* and *Present over Perfect.*

TREVOR NOAH, p. 169: Trevor Noah is the host of the Emmy- and Peabody Award–winning *The Daily Show* on Comedy Central. *The Daily Show* recently received three 2018 Primetime Emmy Award nominations, including Outstanding Variety Talk Series, Outstanding Interactive Program, and Outstanding Short Form Variety Series. In November 2016, Trevor released his first book, *Born a Crime: Stories from a South African Childhood,* which was an instant *New York Times* best-seller. In addition to writing, producing, and starring in multiple comedy specials, Trevor's success has also spanned to sold out shows over five continents.

JOEL OSTEEN, pp. 68–69, 114, 133: Joel Osteen is the senior pastor of America's largest congregation, Lakewood Church in Houston, Texas. His televised messages are seen by more than ten million viewers each week in the United States, and millions more in one hundred nations around the world. His SiriusXM Satellite Radio channel and millions of social media followers have prompted

numerous publications to name him as one of the most influential Christian leaders in the world. He is the author of nine *New York Times* best-sellers, including his two most recent works, *The Power of I Am* and *Think Better, Live Better: A Victorious Life Begins in Your Mind.*

JORDAN PEELE, p. 166: Jordan Peele is a writer, producer, and director. He was the costar and cocreator of *Key & Peele* on Comedy Central. During its five-year run, the hit series garnered more than one billion hits online, received twelve Emmy Award nominations, and won a Peabody Award. Peele's directorial feature debut, *Get Out,* earned four Academy Award nominations, including Best Director and Best Picture, and won him the Oscar for Best Original Screenplay.

WINTLEY PHIPPS, p. 40: World-renowned vocal artist Wintley Phipps is also a pastor, motivational speaker, and author of *Your Best Destiny: Becoming the Person You Were Created to Be.* He is the founder, president, and CEO of the U.S. Dream Academy, a national after-school program that aims to break the cycle of intergenerational incarceration by giving children the skills and vision necessary to lead productive and fulfilling lives.

DANIEL PINK, p. 96: Daniel Pink is the author of five books about business, work, and behavior, including two *New York Times* best-sellers: *A Whole New Mind* and *To Sell*

Is Human. His articles and essays have appeared in *The New York Times,* the *Harvard Business Review, The New Republic,* and *Slate.* Daniel's TED Talk on the science of motivation is one of the ten most-watched TED Talks of all time.

———

SIDNEY POITIER, p. 181: Sidney Poitier is an actor, film director, author, and diplomat. In 1964, Mr. Poitier became the first black actor to win an Academy Award for Best Actor for his role in *Lilies of the Field.* In 2002, he was chosen by the Academy of Motion Picture Arts and Sciences to receive an Academy Honorary Award, in recognition of his "remarkable accomplishments as an artist and as a human being." On August 12, 2009, Mr. Poitier was awarded the Presidential Medal of Freedom.

———

STEVEN PRESSFIELD, p. 65: Steven Pressfield is the author of many books including *Gates of Fire, Tides of War, Last of the Amazons, The Profession, The Lion's Gate, The War of Art, The Warrior Ethos, The Authentic Swing,* and *The Knowledge.* His debut novel, *The Legend of Bagger Vance,* was adapted for the screen.

———

AMY PURDY, p. 56: Amy Purdy is one of the top-ranked female adaptive snowboarders in the world, a three-time World Cup Para snowboard gold medalist, the 2014 Paralympics bronze medalist, and the 2018 Paralympics silver medalist. Amy is the founder of Adaptive Action Sports,

a nonprofit organization that helps youth, young adults, and wounded veterans with physical disabilities get involved with action sports. Her memoir, *On My Own Two Feet,* was published in 2014 and became a *New York Times* best-seller.

———

SHONDA RHIMES, p. 111: Shonda Rhimes is the creator of *Grey's Anatomy* and *Scandal* as well as founder of Shondaland, which produces *How to Get Away with Murder, For the People,* and *Station 19.* For her collective works, Shonda has received numerous honors including a Golden Globe, the Peabody Award, and lifetime achievement awards from the Directors Guild of America, Writers Guild, and Producers Guild. Shonda was also inducted into the Television Academy of Arts & Sciences Hall of Fame. In 2017, Shonda made an unprecedented move to Netflix, where Shondaland will now produce content exclusively for the streaming media company. She is the author of the *New York Times* best-selling *Year of Yes.*

———

ROBIN ROBERTS, p. 185: Robin Roberts has been the coanchor of ABC's *Good Morning America* since 2005. During her tenure, the broadcast has won four Emmy Awards and the 2017 People's Choice Award for Favorite Daytime TV Hosting Team. Roberts founded her own production company, Rock'n Robin Productions, which creates original broadcast and digital programming for ABC and other networks. Roberts is the author of *From the Heart: Seven*

Rules to Live By and her memoir, *Everybody's Got Something.*

FATHER RICHARD ROHR, pp. 125, 178: Father Richard Rohr is a globally recognized ecumenical teacher and founder of the Center for Action and Contemplation in Albuquerque, New Mexico. Father Rohr's teaching is grounded in the practices of contemplation and self-emptying, expressing itself in radical compassion, particularly for the socially marginalized. Father Rohr is also the author of numerous books, including his most recent, *The Divine Dance: The Trinity and Your Transformation.*

CAROLE BAYER SAGER, p. 97: Carole Bayer Sager's songbook spans almost fifty years and contains some of the world's most popular and successful songs. Honors for her work include an Academy Award, a Grammy Award, two Golden Globes, and a Tony Award. Her *New York Times* best-selling memoir, *They're Playing Our Song,* was released in 2016.

DANI SHAPIRO, p. 50: Dani Shapiro is the best-selling author of the memoirs *Still Writing, Devotion,* and *Slow Motion* and five novels, including *Black & White* and *Family History.* Her work has appeared in *The New Yorker, Elle, The New York Times Book Review,* the *Los Angeles Times,* and the op-ed pages of the *New York Times* and has been broadcast on *This American Life.* Dani has taught in the writing programs at Columbia University,

New York University, the New School, and Wesleyan University, and she is a contributing editor at *Condé Nast Traveler.* Her most recent book is *Inheritance: A Memoir of Genealogy, Paternity, and Love.*

MICHAEL SINGER, pp. 78–79: Michael Singer is the author of the number one *New York Times* best-seller *The Untethered Soul.* In 1975, he founded Temple of the Universe, a yoga and meditation center. Michael is also the creator of a leading-edge software package that transformed the medical practice management industry. His latest book is the *New York Times* best-seller *The Surrender Experiment: My Journey into Life's Perfection.*

BROTHER DAVID STEINDL-RAST, p. 115: Brother David Steindl-Rast is a Catholic Benedictine monk, notable for his active participation in interfaith dialogue and his work on the interaction between spirituality and science. He's the cofounder of gratefulness.org, supporting ANG*L (A Network for Grateful Living). He is the author of *Gratefulness, The Heart of Prayer,* and *Deeper Than Words.* His most recent book is *99 Blessings,* a series of prayers for the general reader.

GLORIA STEINEM, p. 139: Gloria Steinem is a writer, speaker, activist, and feminist organizer. She cofounded *New York* Magazine and *Ms.* Magazine, where she remains a consulting editor. She has produced a documentary on child abuse for HBO, a film about the death penalty for Lifetime, and *Woman*, a series of documentaries for Viceland about violence against women in eight countries. She is also the subject of *The Education of a Woman*, a biography by Carolyn Heilbrun, and HBO's *Gloria: In Her Own Words*. Her books include the best-sellers *My Life on the Road, Revolution from Within, Outrageous Acts and Everyday Rebellions, Moving Beyond Words*, and *Marilyn: Norma Jean*. She was a member of the Beyond Racism Initiative, a three-year effort to compare racial patterns in South Africa, Brazil, and the United States. She cofounded and serves on the boards of the Women's Media Center, Equality Now, and Donor Direct Action, and is an adviser to Time's Up, part of a global movement against sexual harassment and violence. In 2013, President Obama awarded her the Presidential Medal of Freedom.

BRYAN STEVENSON, p. 139: Bryan Stevenson is a lawyer, social justice activist, speaker, founder and executive director of the Equal Justice Initiative, and a clinical professor at the New York University School of Law. He wrote the critically acclaimed book *Just Mercy: A Story of Justice and Redemption*, which was selected by *Time* magazine as one of the "10 Best Books of Nonfiction" for 2014.

TIM STOREY, pp. 18, 71: Tim Storey is an acclaimed author, speaker, and life coach. He is well-known for inspiring and motivating people from all walks of life, from executives, celebrities, and athletes to underserved adults and children. Tim is a best-selling author of several books, including *Comeback & Beyond: How to Turn Your Setbacks into Comebacks*, and is the founder of the Congregation, a multi-denominational church based in Placentia, California.

CHERYL STRAYED, pp. 54, 97, 128: Cheryl Strayed is the author of the number one *New York Times* best-seller and Oprah's Book Club selection *Wild*, which became a top-selling feature film and garnered Reese Witherspoon an Oscar nomination for her starring role in the adaptation. Cheryl is also the author of the *New York Times* best-sellers *Tiny Beautiful Things* and *Brave Enough*, and also the novel *Torch*. She's a cohost of the popular advice podcast *Dear Sugar Radio*. Her essays have been published in *The Best American Essays, The New York Times*, the *Washington Post Magazine*, and *Vogue*, among others.

BARBARA BROWN TAYLOR, pp. 21, 168: Barbara Brown Taylor is a *New York Times* best-selling author, teacher, and Episcopal priest. Her fourteenth book is *Holy Envy: Finding God in the Faith of Others*. Her other titles include the *New York Times* best-seller *An Altar in the World, Leaving Church*, and *New York Times* best-seller *Learning in the Dark*. She lives on a working farm in rural northeast Georgia with her husband, Ed.

JUSTIN TIMBERLAKE, p. 112: Multi-talented actor and musician Justin Timberlake has sold more than 32 million albums worldwide, has sold out arenas all across the globe, and has become one of the most highly respected entertainers in the business. His four-time Platinum-selling song "Can't Stop The Feeling!" debuted at number one on the Billboard Hot 100 and was the best-selling U.S. single for 2016. Additionally, it marked Timberlake's tenth Grammy Award and garnered nominations for an Academy Award and a Golden Globe. Timberlake has appeared in diverse films, including *Alpha Dog, Black Snake Moan,* and *Shrek the Third.* He won strong reviews for his performance in the Academy Award–nominated *The Social Network.* Timberlake also has won four Emmy Awards for his appearances on *Saturday Night Live.*

ECKHART TOLLE, pp. 113, 122: Eckhart Tolle is a spiritual teacher and author who was born in Germany and educated at the Universities of London and Cambridge. He is the author of the number one *New York Times* best-seller *The Power of Now* and the highly acclaimed follow-up *A New Earth,* which are widely regarded as two of the most influential spiritual books of our time.

DR. SHEFALI TSABARY, pp. 19, 71: Dr. Shefali Tsabary is the *New York Times* best-selling author of *The Conscious Parent* and *The Awakened Family.* Shefali is a clinical psychologist who helps her clients using a blend of Eastern mindfulness and Western psychology. Her life's mission is to revolutionize the way we raise our children and thereby help heal the planet.

LYNNE TWIST, pp. 146, 160–161: For more than forty years, Lynne Twist has been a recognized global visionary committed to alleviating poverty, ending world hunger, and supporting social justice and environmental sustainability. Her acclaimed book *The Soul of Money: Transforming Your Relationship with Money and Life* was rereleased in April 2017.

CICELY TYSON, p. 158: Cicely Tyson is an Academy Award and Golden Globe Award nominee. She has received three Primetime Emmy Awards, a Tony Award, and a Screen Actors Guild Award. She is the recipient of the NAACP's highest honor, the prestigious Spingarn Award. In 2016, Ms. Tyson was awarded the Presidential Medal of Freedom, the highest civilian honor in the United States.

IYANLA VANZANT, pp. 66–67, 87: Iyanla Vanzant is a six-time *New York Times* best-selling author and among the most influential and acclaimed speakers and spiritual life coaches. Executive producer and host of *Iyanla: Fix My Life* on OWN, Iyanla has inspired millions around the world with her focus on faith, empowerment, and loving relationships. She has authored nineteen books, and her work has been translated into more than twenty-three languages.

KERRY WASHINGTON, p. 58:
Emmy- and Golden Globe–nominated
Kerry Washington starred as Olivia
Pope in the groundbreaking Emmy- and
Peabody Award–winning drama *Scandal*.
As an activist, Kerry was appointed by
President Barack Obama to the President's
Committee on the Arts and Humanities.
She also is an active member of the
V-Counsel, an esteemed group of advisers
to V-Day, the global movement to end
violence against women and girls.

———————————————

JEFF WEINER, pp. 94, 168: Jeff Weiner
is the CEO of LinkedIn, the world's
largest and most powerful network of
professionals. Jeff joined the company in
December 2008; under his leadership,
LinkedIn has grown from 338 to over
12,000 employees in 30 offices around the
world, grown its membership base from 33
million to more than 560 million members,
and increased its revenue from $78 million
to more than $5 billion. Jeff also serves
on the board of directors for Intuit Inc.,
DonorsChoose.org, and Everfi, where he
is codeveloping a program to help ensure
compassion is taught in every primary
school in the U.S. He also sits on the board
of trustees for the Paley Center for Media.

———————————————

**MARIANNE WILLIAMSON, pp. 95,
109, 142:** Marianne Williamson is an
internationally acclaimed author and
lecturer. Seven of her twelve books have
been *New York Times* best-sellers and four
were number one. The mega-best-seller
A Return to Love is considered a must-read
of the New Spirituality. Her most recent
books include *The Twentieth Anniversary Edition
of Healing the Soul of America* and *A Politics
of Love: The Handbook for a New American
Revolution*. In 1989, she founded Project
Angel Food, a program that serves meals to
homebound people with AIDS in the Los
Angeles area. Marianne also cofounded the
Peace Alliance.

———————————————

WILLIAM PAUL YOUNG, pp. 170–171:
William Paul Young is the author of the
number one *New York Times* best-selling
book *The Shack*, which was also made into
a major motion picture in 2017. His other
works include *Cross Roads, Eve,* and *Lies We
Believe About God*.

———————————————

GARY ZUKAV, pp. 89, 149, 187:
A master spiritual teacher and author of
four consecutive *New York Times* best-sellers,
Gary Zukav and his seminal book, *The
Seat of the Soul,* led the way to seeing the
alignment of the personality and the soul
as the fulfillment of life. The book was a
number one *New York Times* best-seller for
thirty-one weeks and remained on the *New
York Times* best-seller list for three years.
Gary and his wife and spiritual partner,
Linda Francis, cofounded the Seat of
the Soul Institute, dedicated to assisting
people across the world in the creation of
authentic power.

ABOUT THE AUTHOR

OVER THE COURSE of her esteemed career, Oprah Winfrey has created an unparalleled connection with people around the world. As host and supervising producer of the top-rated, award-winning *The Oprah Winfrey Show*, she entertained, enlightened, and uplifted millions of viewers for twenty-five years.

Her continued accomplishments as a global media leader and philanthropist have established her as one of the most influential and admired public figures in the world today.

IMAGE CREDITS

Ruven Afanador: Cover, 17, 188
Melissa Gidney Daly: 2, 53, 57, 87, 96, 133, 177
Scott Markewitz: 55, 111, 160–161
Jamie Out: 40 41, 88, 127, 149

pp. 6–7: iStock.com/UWMadison, pp. 8–9: Willowpix/Getty Images, pp. 12–13: Space Images/Getty Images, p. 19: Matt Tomlins/EyeEm/Getty Images, p. 21: Rosmarie Wirz/Getty Images, p. 22: Sergey Makashin/Offset.com, p. 23: andipantz/Getty Images, p. 24: Rolf Vennenbernd/AFP/Getty Images, pp. 26–27: Anton Petrus/Getty Images, p. 30: Pixel Stories/Stocksy United, p. 31: Sylvia Westermann/Getty Images, p. 33: masahiro Makino/Getty Images, pp. 34–35: David Clapp/Getty Images, p. 36: Evgeni Dinev Photography/Getty Images, p. 38: Dani Pfister/500px/Getty Images, pp. 42–43: Ryan Etter/Getty Images, p. 46: Gary Yeowell/Getty Images, p. 47: Cavan Images/Getty Images, pp. 48–49: David Wall/Alamy Stock Photo, p. 51: Josh Boes/Getty Images, p. 52: oluolu3/Getty Images, p. 58: aydinmutlu/Getty Images, pp. 60–61: James O'Neil/Getty Images, p. 65: Michael Okimoto/Getty Images, pp. 66–67: Danny Hu/Getty Images, pp. 68–69: JGI/Tom Grill/Getty Images, p. 70: Anna Xíou Wacker/Getty Images, pp. 72–73: Maya Karkalicheva/Getty Images, pp. 74–75: Aaron Foster/Getty Images, p. 77: Roksana Bashyrova/Getty Images, pp. 78–79: R A Kearton/Getty Images, pp. 80–81: Karl Tapales/Getty Images, pp. 82–83: A330Pilot/Getty Images, pp. 90–91: Anton Petrus/Getty Images, p. 93: Yustinus/Getty Images, p. 95: Doug Berry/Getty Images, p. 98: Crazy Photons/Getty Images, pp. 100–101: Tyler Hulett/Getty Images, p. 103: fhm/Getty Images, pp. 104–105: Mario Gutiérrez/Getty Images, p. 109: Danita Delimont/Getty Images, p. 110: Matteo Colombo/Getty Images, p. 113: Aris Kurniyawan/EyeEm/Getty Images, p. 114: Xuanyu Han/Getty Images, pp. 116–117: Wavebreak Media/Offset.com, p. 123: Peter Zelei Images/Getty Images, p. 124: levente bodo/Getty Images, p. 126: Bryan Dale/Stocksy United, p. 128: I love Photo and Apple./Getty Images, p. 130: Sungmoon Han/EyeEm/Getty Images, pp. 134–135: Paola Cravino Photography/Getty Images, p. 138: Marcel Mendez/EyeEm/Getty Images, p. 140: WIN-Initiative/Neleman/Getty Images, p. 141: Ignacio Palacios/Getty Images, p. 143: Craig Thomson/EyeEm/Getty Images, pp. 144–145: Anton Repponen/Getty Images, p. 146: André Schulze/Getty Images, pp. 150–151: Akepong Srichaichana/Getty Images, pp. 152 153: Marco Bottigelli/Getty Images, p. 157: Julia Jach/EyeEm/Getty Images, p. 159: DieterMeyrl/Getty Images, pp. 162–163: Malorny/Getty Images, p. 165: Sean Gill/EyeEm/Getty Images, p. 167: Raimund Linke/Getty Images, p. 168: Kevin Smith/Design Pics/Getty Images, pp. 170–171: Robert Harding World Imagery/Offset.com, pp. 172–173: Supoj Buranaprapapong/Getty Images, p. 179: Bill Hatcher/Getty Images, p. 180: simon's photo/Getty Images, p. 182: Chris Axe/Getty Images, p. 184: RJW/Getty Images, p. 185: Raimund Linke/Getty Images, p. 187: Kacey Klonsky/Getty Images

CREDITS AND ACKNOWLEDGMENTS

This book was produced by:

MELCHER MEDIA

124 West 13th Street
New York, NY 10011
www.melcher.com

Founder and CEO: Charles Melcher
Vice President and COO: Bonnie Eldon
Production Director: Susan Lynch
Executive Editor and Producer: Lauren Nathan
Project Editor: Victoria Spencer
Assistant Designer and Editor: Renée Bollier

THE AUTHOR WOULD LIKE TO THANK: Oprah Winfrey
Network and Discovery Communications, Inc. Gratitude to the teams
at Flatiron and Melcher Media.

MELCHER MEDIA WOULD LIKE TO THANK: Chika Azuma, Jess
Bass, Amélie Cherlin, Sharon Ettinger, Shannon Fanuko, Julia Hawkins,
Dave Kang, Karolina Manko, Anya Markowitz, Emma McIntosh, Nola
Romano, Gabrielle Sirkin, Chris Steighner, Nadia Tahoun, Megan
Worman, Katy Yudin, and Gabe Zetter.